A Natural Afterlife Discovered

A Natural Afterlife Discovered

The Newfound, Psychological Reality That Awaits Us at Death

BRYON EHLMANN

KAMP
K. Alvin Marie Publishing

LOCAL 133.9013 EHL
2029 6573 10/6/23 NEB
Ehlmann, Bryon.

A natural afterlife discovered

Copyright © 2022 Bryon K. Ehlmann
All rights reserved.

ISBN 979-8-218-11762-7 (paperback)

ISBN 979-8-218-17581-8 (hardback)
Library of Congress Control Number: 2023907436

Published in the United States of American by
K. Alvin Marie Publishing

v 230420

Sunset photo on the cover by Frank Mckenna on Unsplash.com

Cover design by Babski Creative Studios and Bryon Ehlmann

iv

To Barbara
my wife, partner, and best friend
for her steadfast love

Table of Contents

Prologue: Our Natural Eternal Consciousness (NEC) 1

Part I. Overview, Discovery, Evidence, Essence, and Aspects   11

1. A Brief Overview of the NEC Theory: An Inkling Into 13
How a Natural Afterlife Is Possible

2. Discovering Death's New Reality: But Why Hadn't 19
Others

    A Eureka Moment at an Opportune Time 20
    The Big Debate on Near-Death Experiences (NDEs) 21
    The Possibility of a Natural Afterlife 25
    The Psychological Reality of Our NEC 30
    The Eventually Timeless Natural Afterlife (Etna) 31
    The Theory of Paused Consciousness in Timelessness (PCT) 32
    Others Close to Discovery: Harry T. Hunt 34

3. Supported by Human Experience 39

    Thought Experiments 39
    Analogies 43

4. Supported by Cognitive Science Principles 47

    Time Perception 49
    Conscious Perception 53

5 The NEC: Grasping Its Elusive Essence 57

    Relativistic, Timeless, Eternal, and Illusionary 59
    Timely Produced and Timewise Distorted 61
    An Illusion, Yet Very Real to the Dying Person 63
    But What Is Reality? 64
    Objections (or Difficulties in Understanding?) 73
    For Philosophy, A New Type of Immortality 78

6 The NEC Theory: Understanding Its Momentous Aspects ... 85

    Provides a Dreamlike and Spiritual NEC 85
    Independent of NDE Explanations 87
    Natural and Religiously Neutral 88
    A Wide Variety of NEC and Afterlife Experiences 88
    A Logically Consistent, Optimal Heaven 94
    A Natural Afterlife Not Guaranteed 97
    Applicable to Other Creatures 97
    Strengthened Validity Via Explanatory Power 99

Part II. Analysis, Formal Definitions, and Validity   **107**

  7. The Lifetime-in-Eternity Model: A Product of Analysis 109
    The Event Level 110
    The Moment Level 115
    Formal Definitions and an Example 119
    A Summary of Concepts and Relationships 123

  8. Validity Via "Proof" by Deduction 127
    Absolute Vs. Empirical Truths, Theory Vs. Hypothesis 127
    The PCT Theory: Statement and "Proof" 130
    The NEC Theory: Statement and "Proof" 133

  9. Validity Via Testability: A Scientific Theory 139
    Verifiable and Falsifiable Before Death 139
    The PCT Theory: Testing 141
    The NEC Theory: Testing 142

Part III. Confronting the NEC Theory   **149**

10. Accepting the Theory 151
    A Challenge to Orthodoxy, Big-time 152
    A Challenge to Publish 154
    Psychological and Theory-Specific Impediments 161
    Evidence of Acceptance Despite Impediments 165

11. Dealing With the Theory: Philosophical and Religious 169
    Viewpoints
    Overcoming Prior Expectations, Beliefs, and Biases 169
    Where I'm Coming From 173
    General Options: A Matter of Faith 184
    Compatibility With Religious Afterlife Teachings 187

12. Appreciating the Theory: Benefits for the Individual 193
    and Society
    Benefits for the Individual 193
    Benefits for Society 196

Epilogue: Death's Newfound Reality 199
References 207
Acknowledgments 217
About the Author 219
Index 221

List of Acronyms

A new concept requires new, descriptive terms. They're often a bit long and often referenced, so the need for acronyms. Those used in this book are listed below, with the main ones in bold.

BF	brain functionality
DFD	data flow diagram
dNDE	distressing near-death experience
ELDV	**end-of-life dream or vision**
eta	**eventually timeless afterlife**
etna	**eventually timeless natural afterlife**
minBF$_{nde}$	minimum brain functionality for NDE
NDE	**near-death experience**
NDEr	near-death experiencer
NDErs	near-death experiencers
NDNIV	nature does nothing in vain
NEC	**natural eternal consciousness**
NEE	never-ending experience
PCT	paused consciousness in timelessness
OBE	out-of-body experience

Prologue
Our Natural Eternal Consciousness (NEC)

I believe it was November or December of 2012 when I woke up from one of my many weird dreams and thought, "Suppose I had never woken up?" Unbelievably, this was the first time I had asked myself this question. It was a eureka moment that began a 10-year odyssey in evolving and publicizing a new theory about death and the afterlife and eventually led me to write this book.

I must warn you. My theory upsets the orthodoxy on death and the afterlife, and my book will likely change your views on both—and thus, perhaps, your views on life. After reviewing it, a highly regarded, retired writer and editor for my local newspaper stated: "I suspect I'll need the rest of my life to fully digest your theory. But it's given me much to think about." Given the alien food for thought you will be asked to digest from this book, I hope you'll read it carefully, contemplatively, and with an open mind.

The Contents. So you can better judge the contents of this book by its cover, I will explain it. As the title states, and surprising as it is to many (including myself), "A Natural Afterlife" has been "Discovered." Its discovery was possible because this afterlife is natural, unlike all others envisioned. That is, it's supported by human experiences and scientific principles. *There's nothing supernatural (i.e., paranormal) about it.* Its name is not an oxymoron.

The discovered afterlife is a spiritual realm that can be perceived as a heaven, hell, purgatory, or some other experience. The hell and purgatory possibilities, while not to be ignored, are not emphasized in this book. Instead, the main focus is on the positive, the discovered heaven. However, it's important to keep in mind that much of what is said about the discovered heaven also applies to the discovered hell, often in the opposite way. It's also important to remember that it's *a* heaven that has been found, which is not being claimed as *the* one and only Heaven. Most likely, in many ways, it's not like the Heaven that you may have been envisioning. Instead, this heaven is a psychologically based, logically consistent, _eventually timeless, natural afterlife_ (etna).

It is "psychologically based" because "it's all in your mind." It is not a place in three-dimensional space. It is within your mind at death and just timelessly lingers on in your consciousness forever. Being psychological, it is subjective, relativistic, and illusionary. It is subjective in that it is as only you perceive it and may even be personalized for you. It is relativistic in that to understand and envision it now as one of the living, you must put yourself into the proper frame of reference, that of a dying person. It is illusionary in that it is not a reality in the material, sensory sense (like this book you are now seeing through your own eyes). It is, however, very real to the dying person. So, throughout this book, I must often ask you to imagine you are this person.

The heaven is also psychologically based in that it's supported by psychological—specifically, cognitive science—principles. This support sets it apart from all other envisioned heavens.

The heaven is "logically consistent," meaning that its features are not contradictory. Heaven, as commonly envisioned, is eternal and perfect, providing free will, joyful happenings, and utmost happiness. A Heaven with such features, however, can be proven to be logically impossible. The features of the discovered heaven, on the other hand, are not contradictory and can provide eternal, utmost happiness. Its logical consistency sets it apart from almost all other envisioned heavens.

The heaven is "eventually timeless," as denoted by the "et" in the acronym etna (pronounced like Mount Etna). Here *timeless* has the common dictionary meaning of "not affected by time" and thus never changing. For you (again, as the dying person), this means that after some time has passed, in which you may have experienced several activities, nothing more happens in this heaven. But don't fret. You will never miss a thing because you will never know that nothing more will ever happen. In fact, you will always believe it will (as is later made clear). Surprisingly, it is the eventually timeless aspect of the discovered heaven that is required to logically provide eternal, utmost happiness.

The heaven is a "natural afterlife," denoted by the "na" in etna, because 1) it's not supernatural, as already explained and 2) while not *after* life, **you** cannot perceive death and so **to you,** it's eternal, like any afterlife. Relativity is the key to understanding it, as is true with the relativity of time, theorized by Einstein. For the heaven is only eternal relative to you (i.e., from your perspective as the dying person). Life for you becomes imperceptibly timeless and deceptively eternal. Though relative to the living, you are only experiencing an illusion, like a rainbow. But from your perspective, the heaven is truly real—which in the end, is what really matters.

As this book will make clear, the etna does not conflict with the supernatural afterlife that you may currently envision. You may continue to believe in it, and if in the end you were wrong, an etna could still be there for you as the natural fallback. Or, after reading this book, you may put your faith in the etna, which can be a heaven of the utmost happiness. Regardless, this choice can be independent of your belief or disbelief in a God because it's unknown what or who determines the kind of etna one may have.

Now I explain how the images on the book's cover relate to the book's subtitle and content. The beach sunset in the brain portion of the head silhouette represents the visual part of a discrete conscious moment within the mind of a person. It is a present moment within the stream of past, present, and future ones that produce human consciousness. If possible, I would have shown the sounds, odors, feelings, and emotions that are also part of this moment. It's not one within this person's natural afterlife as we'll assume they're alive, standing on a real beach. However, it could just as well be a moment within such an afterlife.

The "Consciousness" control panel metaphorically represents how the stream of conscious moments operates for humans. This stream is turned on with an ON button at birth or near birth. It is paused at a particular moment with a Pause button (❚❚) whenever a person falls asleep or passes out. Metaphorically, such a pause is accurate, as explained later in this book. The stream is restarted with a Restart button (▶) whenever a person wakes up or begins an experience when not awake, such as a dream. An OFF button, which would turn off the stream, is finally being eliminated. It has erroneously been on this control panel for centuries.

Metaphorically, there's no such OFF button for human consciousness. For turning off the consciousness stream would lose the present moment like the present picture is lost when pressing OFF to turn off a streaming movie. Such a loss just does not happen with death and thus would *mis*represent it.

Rather, as this book reveals and justifies, based on human experience and cognitive science principles, death only means that the stream of consciousness has been paused—imperceptibly so on a present moment—and the Restart button no longer works. The phenomenon that human consciousness once turned on can never be turned off, but only paused, is the psychological foundation for the discovered "Natural Afterlife" stated in this book's title. It is also the "Newfound, Psychological Reality That Awaits Us at Death," the subtitle of this book.

As I stated before, I began the evolving discovery of this reality when I simply woke up one morning from a dream and imagined that I had never woken up. You never know a dream is over until you wake up. But if you never wake up, how will you ever know the dream is over? Short answer: *You won't!*

The NEC Theory. This book is all about what I came to call the *theory of a natural eternal consciousness* (*NEC*), or *NEC theory* for short—the NEC being the "Newfound, Psychological Reality" referred to in its subtitle. The book is intended to be comprehensive. I don't plan to write another. I tell of my evolutionary path and travails along the way in analyzing, defining, explaining, and making public the NEC—an incredibly long-overlooked phenomenon, which makes possible the etna. Hopefully, I will clarify the fuzzy and brief descriptions of the NEC and etna I've given so you can fully understand them, be convinced of their reality, decide how to deal with them, and perhaps even appreciate them.

Just to be clear from the start, everyone has an NEC. You will be imperceptibly paused in some end-of-life experience—meaning, it will become imperceptibly timeless and deceptively eternal. The NEC is just an illusion to the living, but to you, it's real. Thus no one will return to their non-existence before life. Only some will have an etna—hopefully, a heavenly one.

Near-Death Experiences. A heavenly etna would have been the fate of neurosurgeon Eben Alexander had he not survived his near-death experience (NDE). Briefly, NDEs are powerful, transformative mystical experiences that share some common features and have been reported by many near-death survivors. In October 2012, Alexander published a book about his NDE, *Proof of Heaven: A Neurosurgeon's Journey into the Afterlife* (Alexander 2012a). Within a month, it became the #1 New York Times best-selling nonfiction paperback and remained in the top 10 for months. Almost instantly, many scientists, including neuroscientists, questioned the validity of the medical circumstances of his near-death account and his claim that his NDE was "Proof of Heaven" (e.g., Dittrich 2013). This book addresses this claim.

Indeed, this book can be seen as an unauthorized sequel to Alexander's book and others that are based on a personal account of an NDE. Each of these books tells of the happenings in an NDE up to the time a person recovers. This book explains what would have happened with the NDE had the person not recovered and why.

But Is This Theory Really True? By now, you may be thinking: "How can this author make these claims? Has he died and come back to life"? Well, the author never claims in this book that the NEC theory is *true*. I can't. However, I can and do claim that it's a scientific theory. No scientific theory is considered absolutely true. It can only be considered valid until shown otherwise or in need of being revised. Essentially, a theory attains the status of scientific when it can be and has been verified repeatedly by observation and is capable of being falsified by observation. But how can the NEC theory be verified or falsified unless someone returns from the dead? It can be, as will be shown, because the NEC is present *before* death. One example of another scientific theory is Darwin's theory of evolution by natural selection.

Like Darwin's theory, the NEC theory challenges centuries-old orthodoxy. Thus, many who have encountered it, which now includes you, think it unbelievable. Like evolution, many can't bring themselves to accept it and often dismiss it. Some have scolded me for it. But rest assured, some who truly understand the NEC theory accept it. Indeed, three articles I've written related to it have been published in scholarly psychology journals. After reading a draft of my first article, the author of a classic book on NDEs and head of a major NDE research foundation stated:

PROLOGUE

> I hope your article is published because it is a fascinating new line of thinking about the afterlife. I see no flaws in my brief review.

After reviewing the submitted article, the editor of the journal that published it, a philosopher and consciousness scholar, stated:

> I've received a fair number of papers dealing with the NDE and—in spite of the unique direction you've taken—yours is by far the most comprehensive, the most fair-minded, and, frankly, the most extraordinary ....

And finally, after reviewing my second article, the editor of the journal that published it, a psychology scholar, stated:

> Wow! I'm a bit speechless. ... my "wow" pertained to the writing and topic, everything.[1]

The Author. Now that I've told you about the contents of this book and the theory it presents, I'll tell you a bit about its author. I am a retired computer science professor, and as such, I practiced software engineering and taught it. My background is reflected in my analysis and the software engineering tools I use in Part II. These tools are the best means that I know of to develop a deeper understanding of a new phenomenon related to some system—in this case, the NEC and the human mind, respectively.

Now you may wonder, "What credibility does a computer scientist have in claiming a new *psychological* reality (or phenomenon) about death?" My response is that I would have likely never discovered the reality had I been, say, a psychology professor. If I had, I probably would've thought like one—overly concerned with testing any hypothesis before daring to seriously consider and thoroughly analyze it and not wanting to stray too far outside the mainstream of psychology. This mindset is one reason, I believe,

---

[1] The individuals quoted in the Prologue are named in either Chapter 10 or the Acknowledgments.

that the natural afterlife—though seemingly, cognitively obvious—has been overlooked by many thousands of psychologists (an opinion I justify more in Part III). In his #1 NY Times Bestseller, *Range: Why Generalists Triumph in a Specialized World*, David Epstein (2019), gives reasons for and much anecdotal evidence supporting the fact that innovation in a specialized field often must and does come from someone outside the field.

I am a theoretically minded person who tends to "think outside the box." I'm also inquisitive, analytical, and logical. As a computer scientist, I don't hypothesize and immediately think, "How do I test this?" Instead, after some analysis, I hypothesize an idea, often a software solution, and then precisely model and define it with more research and analysis. The next step is to implement the solution by designing and developing computer programs while logically proving them correct. Only then comes testing, not so much to validate the hypothesis but to find errors in the solution's definition and development.

Besides being theoretical and analytical, I believe two other factors facilitated my natural afterlife discovery. First, I'm open-minded about religion and the afterlife and thus unimpeded by strong biases. Second, I retired early, at sixty-two, and could refocus my research on dreams, NDEs, death, and the specific cognitive principles that formed the bases of the NEC theory.

Organization. The book is divided into three parts. The prime objective of Part I is to explain the NEC and etna so that, hopefully, you'll develop a good understanding of these phenomena and perhaps accept their reality. I informally explain them with ever-increasing levels of detail, which has already begun with this prologue. A second objective is to tell a bit about myself and the evolution of how I unbelievably came to discover and understand the NEC and etna. I say "unbelievably" because I remain amazed that someone else didn't discover it earlier (although within the book, I offer some speculations as to why).

Part II of the book presents an in-depth analysis of the NEC. Its first objective is to formally define the NEC and etna. The definitions are based on an abstract model of the various states of consciousness and timelessness that we transition in and out of before, during, and after our lifetime. Its second objective is to validate the NEC theory as a scientific theory by logically deducing it and showing that it has been and can further be tested before death.

Part II gets a bit technical, even mathematical in a few places. It can be skipped by the less technically inclined; however, I encourage everyone to give it a try. By perusing diagrams and following arrows, you will develop a deeper understanding of the NEC and consciousness in general. Also, you may learn some valuable tools that computer scientists and software engineers use for analyzing and describing systems, processes, languages, and vocabularies but which have broader applications. An example is their use in psychology, which is demonstrated in this book.

Part III of the book gives my views on the significance and impacts of the NEC. I point out the problems I've faced in getting others to accept its reality—caused, I think, by its elusive essence and profound implications and the difficulty in challenging the long-held orthodoxy concerning death. I also discuss options as to how one can deal with it. I address aspects of the NEC that may require one to rethink their current philosophical and religious views and, after disclosing my religious beliefs, examine the possible compatibility of the NEC and etna with the afterlife teachings of major religions. Lastly, I indicate how one can appreciate the NEC by pointing out its benefits for individuals and society—hopefully improving both, mutually and gradually over time.

I conclude the book with a summary and some final thoughts in an epilogue.

Part I
Overview, Discovery, Evidence, Essence, and Aspects

It's all in your mind.

—Anonymous

In this first part, I try to explain everything you need to know about the psychological reality that awaits you at death and how I came to realize this reality and understand its elusive essence and important aspects. I don't get into the technicalities of analysis, formal definition, deduction, and testing that formally define and validate this reality, which you can find in Part II, or discuss its psychological, philosophical, and religious impacts and significance, which you can find in Part III. But I delve below the surface into its essence and relate it to reality as well as current philosophical teachings on death and immortality.

Chapter 1

A Brief Overview of the NEC Theory
An Inkling Into How a Natural Afterlife Is Possible

> *To be, or not to be, that is the question: ... to die, to sleep no more; and by a sleep, to say we end the heart-ache, and the thousand natural shocks that flesh is heir to? To sleep, perchance to dream; aye, there's the rub, for in that sleep of death, what dreams may come, when we have shuffled off this mortal coil, must give us pause.*
> —William Shakespeare, *Hamlet*, Act III, Scene I

As expressed in Hamlet's soliloquy, wherein he ponders suicide, Shakespeare (or at least Hamlet) had it right about death and dreams. He just didn't provide the psychological basis and the details for precisely how "dreams may come" in "that sleep of death." He sees death as merely a very long sleep and, as such, believes that "dreaming while dead" is possible. Death is indeed like sleeping in that a period of timelessness is encountered wherein nothing new is perceived; nothing further happens. However, in sleep (and after passing out), this timelessness can be interrupted by dreams. But in death? Well, likely not; however, dreams can be interrupted by the onset of death, in which case the dreamer never awakes. Now, if the dreamer never awakes and "nothing further is perceived" within the ensuing timelessness of death, then how does the dreamer ever know that the dream is over? They don't. Therefore, indeed "in that sleep of death ... dreams may come," but when they do, they come just *before* death and in the mind of the dying person—*i.e., from their perspective*—the dream just lingers on *after* death, unknowingly paused in time and seemingly forever. So just imagine what will happen if you never wake up from a dream. In life, you have never experienced this, but with death, as Shakespeare suggests, you may.

For centuries humans have considered just two main possibilities for what awaits us at death: 1) a "nothingness" like that of our before-life (i.e., the period before life) or 2) some supernatural afterlife. These possibilities summarize the orthodoxy concerning death. They have been the only positions available in an age-old public debate and a personal private one. But finally, a new reality about death has been discovered. Perhaps, however, I should say "uncovered" because I feel this reality was just lying there like a lump under a blanket just waiting for someone to lift the heavy blanket of orthodoxy to uncover it.

The reality is that when you die, assuming no supernatural afterlife, things will not be, from your perspective, as they were before you were born. Instead, you will be timelessly, though imperceptibly so, and eternally, though deceptively so, paused in the last conscious moment of your final experience. These two sentences, plus another to be given below, essentially state the *theory of a natural eternal consciousness* (*NEC*), or *NEC theory* (Ehlmann 2020, 57-62). I state them emphatically and boldly because, given centuries-old orthodoxy and people's deep-seated views on an afterlife, I have found that this new reality can be so hard to understand and accept for many. For those who do, it can be even harder to deal with. And for many others, it can be hard to appreciate.

Admittedly, the NEC theory is difficult to understand and accept. To do so, one must put themselves into the mind of a dying person and completely ignore what they now know is happening materially but when dying is imperceptible to them. If one can do this—i.e., maintain only the dying person's perspective—the NEC as a psychological phenomenon and illusion should be obvious.

By *dying person*, I mean throughout this book, someone who is not only dying but then dead because at death, which is imperceptible, one never knows the difference. So, imagine you are this person.

Yes, after your *final* conscious (i.e., perceived) moment, your brain cells will imperceptibly die and all brain function will cease. Like all the other discrete moments that produce our stream of consciousness, this final moment is timeless (i.e., unchangeable). It's a static "snapshot" of an experience at a point in time, yet you don't *perceive* it as timeless. But more than a snapshot, it includes your sense of self and all other senses, an awareness of the experience, your feelings and emotions, and the anticipation of more consistent moments to come and thus a sense of time and more life (at least for a few moments). With death, you will never perceive another moment to supplant the final present moment from your consciousness or others that can dim its remembrance. Thus, it will *seem* eternal to you, yet in reality, it is not. Given both the imperception and deception of material reality occurring in your mind, your NEC will be an illusion, an *end-of-life illusion of immortality*.

And if the beach moment on the book's cover is your last? Perhaps in a dream? Then, you will delight in the seagulls flying, the waves crashing, and the sea breezes blowing *forever in your mind*.

Thus, ironically, the NEC is possible not because some supernatural consciousness continues after death but because all mortal material-based consciousness ends just before death. After your last conscious moment of your final experience, the death of brain cells will allow nothing more to be *consciously* perceived—no indication to you at or near the moment of death that you've died, no "The End" will be perceived. Your last moment becomes your forever present, with future like-moments always anticipated.

This present may be in an end-of-life dream or vision (ELDV) or near-death experience (NDE)—heavenly, hellish, or something in between. Vivid and meaningful ELDVs, where the "V" for vision is synonymous with hallucination, have been recorded throughout history. Observations by palliative care providers and focused research studies have found them to be very common (Barbato et al. 2017; Chawla et al. 2017; Hoffman 2016; Kerr et al. 2014). The NDE, which is not considered the same as a dream (Long 2003), is a phenomenon evidenced by numerous accounts recorded across cultures and also throughout history as far back as the oral tradition (Holden, Greyson, & James 2009b; Greyson 2021; Moody 2001; Shushan 2022, 18). It occurs in an altered state of consciousness, as do dreams, and is thus dreamlike to some extent, though often much more intense.

You may perceive this ELDV or NDE as an afterlife. This has been the case for many surviving *near-death experiencers (NDErs)* (Masumian 2009). Thus, **the NEC may be a natural afterlife**. This possibility makes the NEC very hard to accept and deal with for those who don't believe in an afterlife.

The natural afterlife is the culmination of an *eventually timeless natural afterlife (etna)*. An etna—again pronounced as in Sicily's Mount Etna—begins at the start of one's final experience, which may include many activities. From the dying person's perspective, this is where their afterlife began because, again, the moment of death is imperceptible to them. Indeed, within their last experience, they may mistakenly believe they have died. What's unique about the etna and the key to understanding it is this: it's not about realizing you're in the afterlife *after* you've died, as humans have always thought, but perhaps believing you're there *before* you've died and never knowing otherwise.

It is important to note that the NEC theory merely states a newfound reality about death that is only relevant "assuming no supernatural afterlife" immediately follows death. Essentially, this new reality implies that a death resulting in complete "nothingness," like that before birth, is simply "not in the cards." Instead, with death, everyone will experience from their perspective, *as the default*, the last moment of their last experience forever, shocking as this may be—*unless* at or sometime after death, a supernatural afterlife overrides it.

Before the NEC theory, a supernatural afterlife was the only kind of hereafter thought possible given current scientific understanding. Now, however, the NEC, perhaps by providence, provides the scientific possibility that death can result in natural eternal peace and contentment and maybe even a natural afterlife of utmost eternal happiness (though, dare I say, there is also the possibility of the flipside to such).

The remaining chapters of Part I: reveal how I came to discover and understand the reality of the NEC and how others have come close; give the evidence for this reality and explain its psychological basis and essence; further explain the NEC theory and its many aspects, including the wide variety of hereafter timeless experiences made possible; address some of the difficulties others have had in understanding the NEC—caused in part, I think, by its elusive essence; contrast the NEC with age-old philosophical views on immortality; and, finally, discuss how the NEC theory gives new meaning to ELDVs and NDEs.

As you read on, however, try not to get too hung up by the intricacies necessary to precisely define the essence and basis of the NEC—i.e., the elusive adjectives and phrases like "timelessly eternal." The simplicity and reality of the NEC, natural afterlife, and etna can be grasped by simply keeping foremost in your mind the question: "If you have an ELDV or NDE just before death, how will *you* ever know it's over?" with the big emphasis on "you." In an early *HubPages* article about the natural afterlife (Ehlmann 2013b), I described the heavenly natural afterlife in a nutshell, as shown in Figure 1.1—literally, to satisfy *HubPages'* desire for figures in its articles.

Note that "believing" requires self-awareness and has no material existence. In Chapters 4 and 5, I discuss the importance of self-awareness in making the NEC and natural afterlife possible.

In subsequent chapters, I describe these two phenomena in different ways—close to the point of redundancy, especially for those who quickly grasp their essence. But I do so because I've found that when one explanation doesn't make sense to someone, another slightly different one sometimes does. Also, one can often gain more insight into a phenomenon by viewing it from different perspectives.

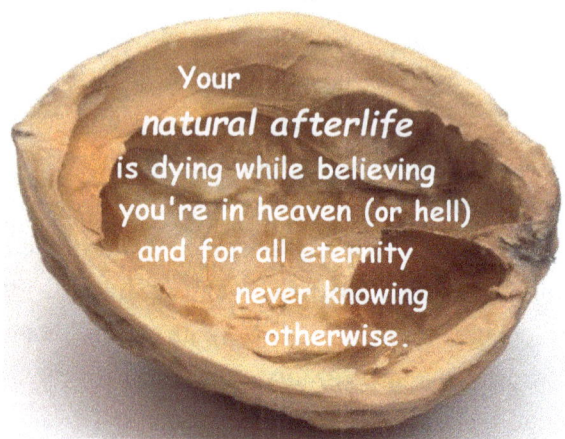

Figure 1.1. A simple description of the heavenly natural afterlife. All but text, © Tsekhmister | Dreamstime Stock Photos & Stock Free Images

Chapter 2

Discovering Death's New Reality
But Why Hadn't Others?

Both heaven and hell are within us.
—Mahatma Gandhi

In this chapter, I answer the question I'm often asked: What led me to realize, uncover, discover, or conceive of the natural afterlife and NEC? I used "discovered" in the title of this book and "discovering" in the title of this chapter. I could have just as well used "realized" and "realizing" or "uncovered" and "uncovering," respectively. However, I would never use "conceived" and "conceiving." This is because I have been accused of, even berated for, *conceiving* the natural afterlife and NEC, which in context meant concocting. I reject these views for I had no motive to concoct them and believe these phenomena describe realities just waiting to be realized, uncovered, or discovered and then named and explained. Indeed, I feel it's the kind of discovery where many will say to themselves, "Why didn't I think of that?"

In conveying how I discovered the natural afterlife, NEC, and etna, which was an evolution of discovery in that order, I give examples of how others, like Shakespeare, have come close to discovering these phenomena. While they envisioned or hinted at part of their essence and perhaps some of their aspects, they did not see and thus precisely define nor describe them completely nor provide the needed scientifically based support for their reality. Specifically, they did not consider the ordinary everyday experiences and the cognitive science principles that provide this support. These are presented in detail in Chapters 3 and 4, respectively.

A Eureka Moment at an Opportune Time

As indicated in the Prologue, I believe it was November or December 2012 when I woke up from a dream and thought, "Suppose I had never woken up?" That eureka moment was the seed for what would eventually become the NEC theory. The fertile ground was the reading I had been doing on NDEs, the time to do research, and an open mind about religion and the afterlife. The nutrients for growth were, I believe, a rational, scientifically inclined, analytical mind; a compulsion to further investigate and analyze; and a tendency to often "think outside the box."

Regarding the fertile ground, 2012 was the first year of my retirement as a professor of computer science from Southern Illinois University Edwardsville. Early retirement at the start of the year had allowed me to redirect my efforts and skills from teaching and research in the fast-paced, hard-to-keep-up-with field of computer science to reading and exploring other areas selectively. I always had a keen interest but little time to explore—cosmology, quantum theory, evolution, religion, and philosophy (especially what I considered the Big Questions).

Now, as to my claim of having an open mind and the "nutrients for growth" that I mentioned, you will have to trust me or decide for yourself based on this book. Regarding the latter, I was a computer science professor and software engineer who taught logic and analytical tools. I often used both to develop computer software systems, databases, user interfaces, and formal languages. The lifetime-in-eternity model, presented in Chapter 7, shows my use of some of these tools, and within this book, I hope you find my logic flawless. Also, my two sisters often accuse me of being *too* analytical and rational. Of course, I always dispute the "too."

The Big Debate on Near-Death Experiences (NDEs)

Before the seed was planted in the Fall of 2012, I happened to come across two articles about NDEs, one published by *Newsweek* and the other by *Scientific American*. A cover article in the October 2012 issue of *Newsweek*, "Heaven is Real" by neurosurgeon Eben Alexander (2012b), discussed his New York Times bestselling book *Proof of Heaven* (2012a). He claimed that his 2008 *near*-death experience was an *after*-death experience—i.e., he had died, gone to Heaven, and then returned to life. I then discovered that many other popular books had been written that, based on an individual's NDE, had also made this claim. One example is *Heaven is for Real: A Little Boy's Astounding Story of His Trip to Heaven and Back* by Todd Burpo (2011). Figure 2.1 shows other examples.

Alexander's claim was soon challenged in an article by science educator Kyle Hill (2012) published on a *Scientific American* blog. It was titled "The Death of 'Near Death': Even If Heaven Is Real, You Aren't Seeing It." Citing neuroscientists, he argued that the Heaven that Alexander experienced most likely "occurred while his brain function was either on the way down or on the way back up." Also, while admitting that the NDE "is real," Hill pointed to scientific evidence that they can occur independent of dying and that the "symptoms of an NDE are scientifically explainable."

A NATURAL AFTERLIFE DISCOVERED

Figure 2.1. A sample of books on NDEs at a bookstore. Each book claimed that NDEs provide proof of a supernatural Heaven.

Wanting to explore NDEs further, I found books published by NDE researchers that supported the claims of Alexander, Burpo, and others. Each is based on studies involving interviews with numerous NDE experiencers, called *NDErs* by these researchers. Examples of such books are *Life after life: The Investigation of a Phenomenon—Survival of Bodily Death* by philosopher, psychologist, and physician Raymond Moody (2001); *Evidence of the Afterlife: The Science of Near-Death Experiences* by physician and radiation oncologist Jeffrey Long (2010); and *Consciousness Beyond Life: The Science of the Near-Death Experience* by cardiologist Pim van Lommel (2010). These books claim that NDEs provide proof or evidence of a supernatural afterlife—i.e., that human consciousness continues after death.

On the other hand, I also found many more published articles, like Hill's, that disputed that NDEs provide proof or even evidence of an afterlife. One such article is "Why a Near-Death Experience Isn't Proof of Heaven" by Michael Shermer (2013). Figure 2.2 lists this article first. Other examples follow in alphabetic order (Choi 2011; Clark 2007; Harris 2012; Lecher 2012; Stenger 2012).

These articles, in popular scientific publications or blogs, point to scientific research showing that the common features of NDEs are explainable as natural physiological responses, which can be replicated by brain stimulations, certain drugs, or diseases. Such responses are believed to be induced by the brain as it senses disaster or goes into shutdown *before death*. Based on this research, the articles claim that NDErs are just mistaking a natural *hallucination* (as some call it) for a supernatural afterlife.

So, who was right? After analyzing both positions on NDEs and the phenomenon of never waking up from a dream *or an NDE*, I decided neither was on target. Both sides in the debate were fixated on the orthodox view of a time-perceiving afterlife, one that would include events (i.e., happenings) and be seen as such from both the perspective of the dead and the living if the latter could just peer beyond the grave. But why did there need to be events in an afterlife, and why couldn't an afterlife be subjective—i.e., something only perceived in a person's mind?

That is, suppose it was *timeless* and *relativistic*. I thought Alexander and others lacked scientific evidence in claiming that the NDE provides "Proof of Heaven"—i.e., a heavenly, event-filled, *after*-death NDE, the last term an oxymoron. But I now also thought Hill and others were wrong in claiming or implying that the NDE provided no *evidence* of an afterlife. Why? Because a *near*-death experience would lead to a timeless and relativistic afterlife when the NDEr never wakes up. So, Alexander and others didn't need to claim an *after*-death NDE, and Kyle Hill was wrong in his subtitle, "Even If Heaven Is Real, You Aren't Seeing It."

Why a Near-Death Experience Isn't Proof of Heaven
in Scientific American

Peace of Mind: Near-Death Experiences Now Found to Have Scientific Explanations
in Scientific American

Has science explained life after death?
in HowStuffWorks

Science on the Brink of Death
by SAM HARRIS

FYI: WHAT CAUSES NEAR-DEATH EXPERIENCES? in POPSCI

Not Dead Experiences (NDEs)
in THE HUFFINGTON POST

Figure 2.2. Examples of scientific articles on NDEs. Each article claimed, based on science, that NDEs provide no evidence of an afterlife.

In the case of a heavenly NDE, like Eben Alexander's, yes, *you* are "Seeing It"! You, the dying person, are indeed seeing it. And if you die, you'll never know that you're no longer seeing it. Thus, and most importantly, you will be seeing it eternally. But it is eternal only *from your perspective*. Also, you will never know that it has become timeless as you will always be anticipating another moment. It is timeless only *from the perspective of the living*. They know it's only a static moment, materially obliterated with death.

The Possibility of a Natural Afterlife

That last paragraph expresses the relativistic and timeless essence of the natural afterlife, both essences utterly foreign to the orthodox view of a Heaven, any kind of heaven, and thus never considered by either side in the NDE debate.

Soon after I had formulated my position on this debate based on a natural afterlife, I read an article by writer and journalist Lisa Miller. With the help of a friend, she envisioned one essence and one aspect of the natural afterlife. In a *Newsweek* article, "Can Science Explain Heaven," she states:

> There are those who believe that science will eventually explain everything—including our enduring belief in heaven. The thesis here is very simple: heaven is not a real place, or even a process or a supernatural event. It's something that happens in your brain as you die. I first encountered this idea as I was researching my new book, *Heaven: Our Enduring Fascination With the Afterlife*. I was having lunch with my friend and colleague Christopher Dickey ... Chris believes that everything we think we know about heaven happens in the moments before death. After that, there's nothing. (Miller 2010)

The idea that heaven "happens in your brain as you die ... in the moments before death" is consistent with the psychological essence and dream-like (perhaps NDE-based) aspect of a natural afterlife but not the statement "After that, there's nothing."

I replied to Miller's thesis in an op-ed I submitted to *The New York Times* in January 2013 and directly to her as follows: "The NED Theory refutes that 'there's nothing' because after death we never know that there's nothing, we just know we're in heaven." To elaborate, when I began writing about the natural afterlife, I called my theory the Never-Ending Dream (NED) theory. Also, though "there's nothing" from the perspective of the living, from the perspective of "we," the dying, "we never know there's nothing" because we never know our last experience has ended. The perspective of the dying is the psychological frame of reference, while that of the living is the material frame of reference. Such is the relativistic essence of the NEC.

My op-ed was rejected, which was not surprising because submitting it to The New York Times meant I was "shooting for the moon." After a few more rejections, I turned the op-ed into my first article on the natural afterlife. I titled it "Perhaps Heaven Is Our Never Ending Dream and Natural Afterlife" (Ehlmann 2013a) and published it in May 2013. In the article, I stated my *theory of a natural afterlife*, or *NED theory* for short, as follows:

> Your *natural afterlife* is a dreamlike, near-death experience (NDE) from which you never awake and thus one that, to your knowledge, never ends.

The "Perhaps" in the title of my article admits that at this point, the NED theory was only conjecture, based mainly on human experience, not a theory in a scientific sense. So, as a retired software engineer, who is a person that investigates whether a new concept related to some system is feasible for implementation, I set about trying to analyze whether the concept of a natural afterlife was "feasible" as a new reality. For the software engineer, this involves systems analysis and modeling, which has these objectives: 1) to better understand the current related system, 2) to better understand the new concept in the context of this system, 3) to more precisely define it within this context, and 4) to determine how the new concept would impact the system, if it makes sense or not, and if it will provide significant improvement given its cost.

In applying this methodology to the concept of the NED theory, the current system to be analyzed and modelled was the "human consciousness system" (i.e., the mind). The "new concept" was the natural afterlife. The applicable parts of the system to analyze were the various states of mind and the types of events perceived and processed within them as well as those events that caused transitions between them. Especially relevant were events that transitioned one between a state of conscious awareness, wherein events are perceived (i.e., time is perceived), and a state wherein events are not perceived (i.e., one of timelessness). Also, since the natural afterlife involves the final moment of life, the moments that make up the events were very relevant.

I began this analysis and modelling, along with studying more about our "consciousness system," before publishing my NED article in May 2013 but did so mostly afterward. It eventually resulted in the *lifetime-in-eternity model*, which I first published in a 2016 article. In Chapter 7, I present this model in detail.

From my study of consciousness, I gained more confidence in and appreciation of the timeless, mind-created afterlife that the theory defined. Incredibly influential was reading *Biocentrism* by Robert Lanza (2009) in March 2014. While I cannot say I buy into all of the biocentric principles advanced in the book, I believe in its central theme: "that ... life and consciousness are fundamental to our understanding of the universe"—i.e., our view of reality (2009, 2). In his chapter "Mystery of Consciousness," he states:

> Perhaps some readers will dismiss this [that the brain creates our physical reality] as nonsense, arguing that there's

no way the brain has the machinery actually to create physical reality. But remember that dreams and schizophrenia (consider the movie *A Beautiful Mind*) prove the capacity of the mind to construct a spatio-temporal reality as real as the one you are experiencing now. (2009, 182)

Merriam-Webster defines "spatiotemporal" as "having both spatial and temporal qualities," meaning it is a three-dimensional space that changes with time. The above quote indicates that, as is the case with the natural afterlife, the mind can create a reality as real as the one you experience when awake. This reality should not be surprising because much of what we experience as reality when awake is only created by the mind and only exists therein. The colors of a rainbow do not exist in the sky, only in our minds. A rainbow is purely subjective. Indeed, there are no colors "out there" beyond our brains, only photons of various radiation frequencies. Other examples of "realities" that exist only in our minds are the sound of a tree falling in the forest, the fragrance of a flower, and the solidity of objects and their type. In reality, objects are 99.9999999% empty space, and their type we recognize only by remembering what we were taught (e.g., "That is a book."). I discuss "What is reality?" in more depth in Chapter 5, where I discuss the essence of the NEC.

Lanza begins Chapter 18 by stating, "To be conscious that we are perceiving ... is to be conscious of our own existence.—Aristotle (384–322 B.C.E.)" In the last moment of our final experience, and thus in our natural afterlife, we are indeed "conscious that we are perceiving" and therefore "conscious of our own existence"—i.e., of self.

In his next chapter, titled "Death and Eternity," Lanza states:

Eternity is a fascinating concept, one that doesn't indicate a perpetual existence in time without end. Eternity does not mean a limitless temporal sequence. Rather, it resides *outside of time* altogether" (2009, 189).

He implies here that an afterlife, though eternal, may not be "a perpetual existence in time" (i.e., full of events), which means it may be timeless—i.e., timelessly eternal. Such is the essence of the natural afterlife and one's "existence" within it. Though Lanza hints of a timeless afterlife as real as that which we perceive when we are awake and perhaps as a product only of the mind, in the remainder of his book, he never explains how such existence is possible.

Initially, my focus was on the "never-ending" subjective nature of dreams and dream-like NDEs when being interrupted by death. This focus is why my 2013 *HubPages* article called the theory of a natural afterlife the Never-Ending Dream or NED theory for short. In a more scholarly 2016 article, "The Theory of a Natural Afterlife: A Newfound, Real Possibility for What Awaits Us at Death," I changed the short name of my theory of a natural afterlife to the *NEE theory,* where NEE was an acronym for never-ending experience (Ehlmann 2016). I did so in recognition that many researchers viewed NDEs, though dreamlike, as experiences distinct from dreams. Also, my thinking was that when followed immediately by death, both ELDVs—which include visions (i.e., hallucinations)—and NDEs would become NEEs and, as such, a natural afterlife. At this point, I only claimed the natural afterlife to be "extremely plausible."

In my 2016 article, I restated the theory of a natural afterlife along with a brief explanatory paragraph as follows:

> *The natural afterlife of an NDE-enabled creature is the NDE from which it never awakes—essentially, a never-ending experience (NEE) relative to the creature's perception.*

The theory defines the natural afterlife, implying its existence by its association with the NDE—a phenomenon evidenced by numerous accounts recorded across cultures and throughout history as far back as the oral tradition. Here, the NDE is assumed to be a *near-death* experience, not an *after-death* experience as some postulate. It occurs in an altered state of consciousness, as do dreams, and is thus dreamlike to some extent. (932)

The article went on to state that "It seems very plausible that such vivid, 'near-death' dreams have been reported as NDEs and with death also result in NEEs." (935)

The Psychological Reality of Our NEC

But then, after yet more research on consciousness and cognition, I better understood the cognitive science principles that caused the natural afterlife. This research made me realize that I needed to extend the kinds of experiences that would become NEEs with death, fashion a more general theory on NEEs, define the natural afterlife as a special kind of NEE, and aptly describe the NEE from the perspective of the living as an illusion. I realized that humans (and perhaps other higher-level creatures) had a natural eternal consciousness. What resulted was the more general NEC theory. It could be logically deduced from human experiences and cognitive principles and established as a scientific theory, making it a reality until shown otherwise. Chapter 8 presents the deduction as a formal "proof," and Chapter 9 justifies the theory as scientific.

My 2020 NEC theory article stated the theory along with a brief explanatory paragraph as follows:

The natural eternal consciousness (NEC) of a creature with human-like time and conscious perception is, relative to the creature's perception, its final conscious moment. The NEC may be perceived as a natural afterlife.

The theory postulates that any type of final conscious moment results in an NEC and can be a natural afterlife depending on the kind of NEE it embodies and how it is perceived. (58)

With the NEC, any final experience can become an NEE. Thus, one's hereafter can range from "near-nothingness" to an optimal heaven (or hell). The next chapter hints at these possibilities and others. I discuss them in more detail in Chapter 6.

After first being posted as a preprint on ResearchGate.net and academia.edu in October 2017, the article "The Theory of a Natural Eternal Consciousness: The Psychological Basis for a Natural Afterlife" (Ehlmann 2020) was finally published in May 2020. I elaborate more on "finally" in Chapter 10.

Now, just to clarify the terminology that I had settled on at this point in the evolution, our NEC (natural eternal consciousness) results in our final experience being an NEE (a never-ending experience). Our NEC—the paused last moment of this experience, which embodies the NEE—may (or may not) be perceived as an afterlife. Thus, not everyone's NEC is a natural afterlife, but every natural afterlife is an NEC. From now on, I no longer use the acronym NEE. Enough acronyms, right? However, two more significant terms and, unfortunately, acronyms were to evolve.

The Eventually Timeless Natural Afterlife (Etna)

My evolving discovery and understanding of the NEC continued with a belated realization of the importance of the final experience in defining the entirety of the afterlife that the NEC makes possible. This realization began with another eureka yet, in reflection, "Duh!" moment. It occurred in the Fall of 2020 when writing an early draft of an article titled "Death's New Reality: Challenging Orthodoxy and Dealing With Our End-of-Life Illusion of Immortality," which later turned into this book. The article included a section (now the last section in Chapter 11) that compared the natural afterlife to the afterlife teachings of some major world religions. These teachings describe an afterlife as having activities, yet the natural afterlife has none.

As previously discussed, ELDVs and NDEs, when followed directly by death, may result in a natural afterlife, which is imperceptibly timeless. However, I realized that, from a dying person's perspective, this afterlife is time-perceiving—i.e., one in which activities and events do indeed occur. They just do so before death within the ELDV or NDE and then imperceptibly end with the timeless natural afterlife.

This realization led me to define an *eventually timeless afterlife* (*eta*), which was always implicit in the NEC theory. I just needed to explicitly identify and emphasize this time-perceiving, though "eventually timeless," afterlife. The eta then led me to the realization and definition of the *eta principle for a perfect afterlife*, which I justify in Chapter 6. It essentially states that an eta is a prerequisite for a perfect afterlife. The eta that concludes with the natural afterlife I then called the *eventually timeless natural afterlife* (*etna*) to distinguish it from any supernatural kind of eta.

Now I could compare religious afterlife descriptions to the etna, which contains events and thus activities, rather than to the natural afterlife, which does not. I defined the eta and etna in the article "The Theory of a Natural Eternal Consciousness: Addendum" (Ehlmann 2022). So, to be clear, when the NEC is perceived as a natural afterlife, it will be the culmination, perhaps the climax, of an etna.

The Theory of a Paused Consciousness in Timelessness (PCT)

I conclude the recounting of my evolving discovery and understanding of the NEC with my final realization. It came when I *thought* I had finished writing this book. In late December 2021, I finally received reviews of the Addendum article (Ehlmann 2022) that I had submitted in late April 2021. There were five reviewers, but despite "Addendum" being in the title and the introduction declaring it as an addendum to Ehlmann (2020), followed by the statement "The reader should consult this article for more explanation, if needed, ...," four of the five reviewers did not bother to read the base article. The fifth admitted to only reading half. Some reviews questioned my use of the word "theory" to describe the NEC theory and deemed evidence for it lacking or its falsifiability not demonstrated. Well, this was not surprising if one read only the addendum article, which I never meant as a "stand-alone." Lucky for me, the editor had read Ehlmann (2020), and I was allowed to resubmit with revisions.

Since I didn't want to include large portions of Ehlmann (2020) in the addendum article, my revisions made the article's dependency on Ehlmann (2020) even more apparent. I also, instead of expanding the section on validity with more replication of Ehlmann (2020), searched for an analogy to justify that the NEC theory was indeed worthy of being called a scientific theory.

So, I read some articles on evolutionary theory and its own evolution, and I investigated more thoroughly the scientific use of the words "theory" and "hypothesis." This research was enlightening and led me to realize that I could better present the validity of the NEC theory by basing it on a more general, more explanatory, and perhaps less controversial theory. This I called the *theory of paused consciousness in timelessness (PCT)*, or *PCT theory* for short. My revised addendum article states it, along with a clarifying statement, as follows:

The consciousness of a creature with human-like time and conscious perception is, relative to the creature's perspective, imperceptibly paused in its last conscious moment during periods of timelessness and resumed with its next conscious moment.

The last conscious moment is not remembered upon resumption of consciousness and need not be as it is still the present; however, soon afterward, it may often be forgotten due to some combination of its being mundane and the creature's attention being immediately focused on subsequent moments and events.

Perhaps you can see how the NEC theory can now be based on this theory. I discuss the CPT theory in this regard much more in Chapters 8 and 9, which discuss the validity of the NEC theory.

I believe the new approach significantly improves the validity of arguments presented in Ehlmann (2020), which shows the value of feedback, any feedback. Even bad reviews based on insufficient knowledge of a topic can tickle the brain to come up with something better. It also shows that theories are not "set in stone" but can evolve in completeness, explanation, and presentation. As I write this paragraph, I have been working on the NEC theory in some form since I woke up from that dream in late 2012. As of this writing, that's now been almost ten years!

Others Close to Discovery: Harry T. Hunt

Despite the articles I had published by the Spring of 2020, relatively few were then aware of the NEC theory. These few apparently did not include neuroscientist Christof Koch, who came close to envisioning the natural afterlife. He concludes his June 2020 *Scientific American* article about NDEs by stating: "Perhaps such ecstatic experiences [NDEs] are common to many forms of death ... The mind, chained to a dying body, visits its own private version of heaven or hell before entering Hamlet's 'undiscovered country from whose bourn no traveler returns.'" (Koch 2020, 75). In an email, I referred Koch to my 2020 NEC theory article and wrote: "... significantly, perhaps with death the mind doesn't just *visit* 'its own private version of heaven or hell' but *remains* there timelessly and eternally, and for once in a lifetime the mind becomes un'chained to a dying body.'"[2] I never received a reply.

While Koch's materialistic view of death didn't allow him to envision a natural afterlife, a psychological one allowed psychologist Harry T. Hunt to envision one some twenty-five years earlier. The remainder of this section acknowledges and credits his work.

In January 2021, I posted a preprint of "Death's New Reality" article on academia.edu, which later evolved into this book. After seeing it, Hunt messaged me about his published speculations on an afterlife that was similar to the natural afterlife. Indeed, in his book *On the Nature of Consciousness: Cognitive, Phenomenological, and Transpersonal Perspectives*, Hunt (1995) envisions a "potential afterlife" (256) with an essence much like that of the natural afterlife. You could say his afterlife is the same as the natural afterlife, except that its essence of timeless eternity is explained and supported differently. Specifically, it doesn't result from a universally pulsed consciousness at death (an NEC).

The remainder of this section gives a detailed discussion of Hunt's afterlife, comparing it to the NEC and natural afterlife. The reader may skip to the last paragraph for a summary if they wish.

Hunt (1995) expresses the essence of reality within both his and the natural afterlife very well. He states, "The 'facts' of our experience [e.g., an NDE] may be 'merely subjective,' but that is ultimately where we all live anyway—within our ongoing experience of the world" (255). The last part of this compound sentence is undoubtedly in accord with biocentrism in its emphasis on the primacy of consciousness. In the same chapter, which he states is

---

[2] In this book, my replies may be sometimes slightly revised to improve on brevity, grammar, or explanation.

"more speculative" (xii), he also expresses the relativistic essence of his and the natural afterlife well when he states (with my translations given in brackets[3]):

> From the perspective of the present cognitive psychology of consciousness, and curiously consistent with various spiritual traditions, death turns out to be a third-person phenomenon only [that of the living]. ... From the first-person perspective [that of the dying], specifically enhanced in presentation states [e.g., mystical experiences or NDEs], we really cannot die. (256)

He expresses both the reality and relativistic essence of his and the natural afterlife when he concludes:

> Pragmatically speaking, with respect to the primacy of experience out of which each of us must live, there is a potential afterlife. To label it illusion presupposes that it is given to us [when dying] to stand outside of our own being and intelligence and make such judgments. In the end, either we respect our basic experience of this world or we don't. (256)

Note that I label the NEC as an illusion only from the perspective of living so that the living can better understand it.

Hunt revisits his afterlife theory seventeen years later in the final subsection of the conclusion to an article on the "Phenomenologies of Mystical States" (Hunt 2012, 24–5). He reasons (again adding my translations in brackets):

> As long as ... each moment of our humanly self-aware consciousness contains ... its perpetually felt sense of "not yet," carrying forward [the anticipation of another conscious moment], ... from a first-person [dying person] point of view, which is all we have in this terminal situation

---

[3] By "translation," I mean explanation using terms I use to explain the NEC.

[death], we indeed cannot die. Here ... "third person" [non-experiencing person] issues of truth versus illusion have become irrelevant phenomenologically [from the perspective of the experiencer]. ... Meanwhile, extrapolating from the near-death literature, experience would become more and more fundamental as physiological arousal attenuates, with a concomitant phenomenal sense of timeless eternity.

Note that a "sense of timeless eternity" stemming from a mystical experience is not present in the NEC. In the NEC (as has been indicated and is made clear in Chapter 4), "eternity" is sensed by the dying, deceptively so; however, its "timeless" essence is not, as it is imperceptible to the dying person.

Also, Hunt's afterlife is produced by and dependent on the presence of subjective feelings of timeless eternity within mystical experiences, rather than more generally resulting at death from the cognitive science principles that support an NEC. Hunt indicates that the afterlife he hypothesizes is based on a "cognitive-phenomenological approach" (252, 253) and transpersonal (i.e., spiritual) psychological studies of classical mysticism applied to NDEs. On the other hand, the natural afterlife is based on the cognitive science principles given in Chapter 4—like our complete lack of awareness outside of our discrete conscious moments and our imperceptible loss of time (based on everyday versus mystical human experiences). Such support allows me to more vigorously claim the reality of an afterlife resulting from a universal NEC.

Nevertheless, despite these differences (terminology definitely included!), I feel that Hunt's afterlife theory lends support to the NEC theory. He shows a different route, to an almost exact realization, taken by someone with a very different scholarly background than my own. His was psychology, phenomenology, and spirituality, while mine was computer science, mathematics, hard science, and in retirement, psychology.

Chapter 3

Supported by Human Experience

The true sign of intelligence is not knowledge but imagination.
—Albert Einstein

The NEC theory is supported by everyday human experiences, which this chapter presents via thought experiments and analogies. The thought experiments focus on experiences that are like the death and dying experience for the purpose of analysis that leads to evidence supporting the NEC. The analogies compare the existence, or nonexistence, of the NEC to an experience similar in some respects in order to infer both are likely similar in another respect. Thus, thought experiments and analogies are closely related.

Thought Experiments

As stated in the Prologue and Chapter 2, it was waking up from a dream and imagining that I had instead died that led me to the possibility of being left in a static state of consciousness at death, which I eventually called the NEC. Without forethought or recognition at the time, I had carried out a simple thought experiment. A thought experiment is carried out only in one's imagination to try to draw appropriate conclusions from one or more imagined scenarios (Brown & Stuart 2018). Each of the five scenarios described below presents a common human experience that provides the basis of a thought experiment. Imagining that you never wake up after each scenario, since you've died, allows you to get a sense of the essence of an NEC. It also provides evidence for its existence.

Scenario 1: You are engrossed in watching a movie. Then, without knowing, you unexpectedly fall asleep without any perceived drowsiness. For you, the movie has been imperceptibly paused. While in reality (for others), it continues. Until you wake up, you still believe you are watching that movie (assuming you don't dream). When you wake up, you're shocked that you fell asleep and that the movie has imperceptibly gone on without you.

But now, suppose you never wake up. In your NEC, you would still believe, since nothing would ever happen to change your awareness, that you are "watching that movie."

Scenario 2: Pick a phrase in each [ ] that is always the one before or after the /.): You are having a [pleasant dream / nightmare]. You are [lying on the beach, engaged in a playful conversation with someone you truly love (but who may now be deceased) / being chased down a dark alley by a large, menacing-looking man with a knife]. You awake emotionally [happy with a smile / terrified in a cold sweat but now extremely relieved it was only a dream].

I repeat a dream scenario here to indicate the range of possibilities and that a dream can arouse emotions just as if it were an awake experience.

Again, suppose you never wake up from this dream. In your NEC, you would still believe, since nothing would ever happen to change your awareness, that you are "lying on the beach, engaged in a playful conversation with someone you truly love" or "being chased down a dark alley by a large, menacing-looking man with a knife." I've said it before, and I repeat it: you never know a dream has ended until you experience an awake moment, but if you never do, what will ever happen to make you think the dream is over?

Scenario 3 (a real, personal one): Recently, I was angry at myself for buying a house on the beach as I saw the waves creep closer and closer to my back patio and realized my home would soon be flooded. I was at this house and very upset when I woke up. Then, to my relief, I realized I didn't own that house; it had only been a dream. But where was I? It took me a while to get my bearings—i.e., to look around, access my memory, and figure out in which of my previous homes I was living. But what if I had never woken up?

I offer this thought experiment to point out the immediate shock and confusion that occurs when one's first awake moment is utterly inconsistent with one's last dream moment. When one awakes, the final dream moment is in their mind as the present, not the past. One does not have to remember it—i.e., access their memory. It's just *there*.

In contrast, as indicated by the scenario above, one has to access their memory to remember their last moment before entering the timelessness just before their last experience, a thought process that takes time. For me, this was the last awake moment just before the timelessness of dreamless sleep before my dream (i.e., the one just before I fell asleep). I had lost this moment as the present because of my dream. (Actually, I don't think I tried to access this moment; instead, I accessed my memory to relate my present surroundings to my current house.)

Scenario 4: You're lying on an operating table being administered general anesthesia. You've been told to count backward from 100.

You're counting "93" then "92" but unknowingly never get to "91." Instead, the next thing you know, you're surprised to find yourself in a recovery room with a nurse beside you.

You never know this pre-op experience is over until you wake up. But again, suppose you never wake up. In your NEC, you would still believe, since nothing would ever happen to change your awareness, that you are at "92," counting backward in that operating room, fully expecting to get to "91."

Evidence suggests that although dreams cannot occur during full general anesthesia, NDEs can (Greyson, Kelly, & Kelly 2009; Hameroff 2017a). This possibility and, more so, the many reports of NDEs from those not under general anesthesia lead to the final thought experiment.

Scenario 5. You are having what will be called your NDE should you recover. In this very profound, all too real experience, you are overcome by incredible feelings of wonder, love, and contentment. You genuinely believe that you have arrived, are experiencing heaven, and are excitedly anticipating the next moment and an eternity of joyful experiences.

If you never wake up, this is your NEC. You perceive nothing more, yet nothing less. Everything else that happens after that is irrelevant to you. Very relevant and *relative only to you*, however, is that the moment described above goes on forever. Your NDE consciousness, your sense of self, and, if one exists, your soul have entered a timeless dimension. You are finally, fully, and forever "living in the moment," the final moment of your NDE. You believe you're in heaven, and for all eternity, you never know otherwise.

The above scenario and commentary depict a heavenly NEC and appear almost verbatim in Ehlmann (2016) to describe the natural afterlife. Indeed, this NEC is a natural afterlife.

It and all of the NECs depicted by the above thought experiments reveal a phenomenon that is relativistic, real, timeless, and eternal. These and other NEC properties, which define its essence, are discussed in Chapter 5.

Analogies

Three analogies are especially helpful in understanding the NEC. The first is a good one. The second and third are faulty but still helpful in understanding the NEC when analyzed for their faults. I discuss the first and second analogies here and the third in Chapter 10.

A faulty (or false) analogy assumes that because two things are alike in one or more respects, they are necessarily alike in some other respect. Sometimes there is one crucial, overlooked difference between the things being compared that "makes a whole world of difference," which is the case for analogies two and three.

The first analogy relates to Scenario 4 of the previous section. One can learn much about the NEC's essence by analyzing general anesthesia in more detail. Indeed, the NEC is analogous to permanent general anesthesia—except, keep in mind that with the NEC, one's final experience is hopefully not that of lying on an operating table. The analogy can help to understand how a time-perceiving consciousness followed by an everlasting timeless unconsciousness creates the NEC. However, as with all the scenarios in the prior section, the analogy offers insight only when analyzed from the experiencer's perspective—here, the person being anesthetized.

So imagine you are this person and note that general anesthesia shares the following characteristics, given in italics, with the NEC:

1. *Your last perceived moment includes the anticipation of more such moments to come.* After saying "92," you anticipate as part of that moment saying "91" in the next moment in the

same room to the same people—even despite knowing that your experience here will soon end in an unconscious state.

2. *Your mind never gets the message that there will be no next moment similar to the last* (e.g., with anesthesia, that "you've passed out"). *So you continue to believe that the next moment will follow from the previous* (e.g., that you will still be in that operating room with those people counting backward from what will be "91").

3. *You never lose your sense of self.* When you wake up from general anesthesia, you never ask, "Who am I?" (which is also true with dreaming and dreamless sleep[4]). As William James (1977, 31–3) eloquently explains (though here merely summarized), "it is *myself, I, or me*" that makes life's "*stream ... of consciousness*" seem continuous to the mind despite many "*interruptions*" (i.e., "*time*-gaps") like a dreamless sleep. About the general anesthesia type of time-gap, Stuart Hameroff, a professor of anesthesiology and psychology and director of the Center for Consciousness Studies at the University of Arizona with over 35 years of administering anesthesia, states, "It's still incredible that they're awake, they go to sleep, and come back the same person. Where do they go?" (Hameroff 2017a) He goes on to state, "we can learn a lot about consciousness from anesthesia."

4. *You lose your sense of time.* Hameroff (2017b) states that patients under full general anesthesia experience no passage of time. *Even if you could experience nothingness, which you cannot, there would be no events and thus no time to do so.*

5. *You do not dream.* Hameroff (2017a) states that patients do not dream under *full* general anesthesia. Dreams are, however, pos-

---

[4] Though some people have dreamed that they were someone else—i.e., that they inhabited the body of another person or even an animal—when they awoke, they knew that it was themself that experienced this.

sible when going into or out of full anesthesia, bringing Scenarios like 2 and 3 into play.

6. *Your memory is taken offline. You are not "remembering" your last conscious moment, and you are not dreaming, so memory fragments need not be accessed* (Lewis 2013). *Not only would accessing your memory (i.e., remembering) take time, but timelessness makes it purposeless.*

7. *Your last perceived moment does not seem timeless, which it is, but simply seems to remain the present.* It will seemingly remain the present forever if the anesthesia never wears off, there is no NDE, and you never wake up.

The second analogy is a very commonly stated one but a false one. It's commonly stated because it expresses one of the two main possibilities in the current orthodoxy concerning death. The analogy is that death is like never being born. That is, the time after our death—which going forward, I will often refer to as the *after-life* (with the hyphen to distinguish it from the afterlife)—is just like our before-life (i.e., the period before birth or near-birth).

If there is no supernatural afterlife, the after-life is indeed like the before-life in that one is in a timeless state. Billions of years pass by "in no time at all" from the perspective of an individual. However, there are two huge "analogy-negating differences." Unlike the before-life, one enters the after-life after some last conscious moment—not knowing it was the last and always expecting an immediate one to follow. Also, unlike the before-life, no event, like birth, ever occurs that would eventually terminate the timelessness, unknowingness, and expectedness.

The third analogy compares death to the forever demise (i.e., shutdown) of a computer. Chapter 5 points out why it is faulty.

Chapter 4

Supported by Cognitive Science Principles

> *It is impossible to be conscious of being unconscious from your own perspective. You cannot be aware of not being aware.*
> —Michael Smith, *The Present*, 2013, p. 2

Human experiences with waking up from timeless states of mind, like general anesthesia, and being surprised when our first awake moment doesn't jibe with our last give support to what we will experience upon death when we never wake up. This fate is a consciousness paused in the last moment of an experience, an NEC. But does psychology support such a pause?

From psychology, one can deduce two opposing hypotheses concerning death. The first is based on the definitions for *mind* and *consciousness* given in many introductory psychology textbooks, and thus the one most high school and college students are exposed to. The second delves a bit deeper and is based on human experience and established cognitive principles concerning time perception and conscious perception.

Hypothesis 1. A psychology textbook by Zimbardo, Johnson, & McCann (2014, 325) states: "The *mind* is the product of the brain," *consciousness* is "the brain process that creates our mental representation of the world and our current thoughts," and "as a process ... is dynamic and continual rather than static." Therefore, when the brain dies, the mind as its product and consciousness as a *brain process* must cease to exist and we will "experience" a kind of nothingness like that before life.

Hypothesis 2. For decades evidence has been mounting that we perceive time as a sequence of events, each evolving one discrete conscious moment at a time, which is the present (Elliott & Giersch 2016). We perceive nothing outside of these moments (e.g., dreamless sleep). Before death, a still-functioning brain produces one last present moment of a perceived event within some experience, perhaps a dream, and then is incapable of ever producing another moment that would cognitively supplant the last one from our consciousness. Therefore, we never perceive and thus are never aware that our final experience is over. So a remnant of consciousness, an experience paused in a moment at a point in time, will become imperceptibly timeless (i.e., *static*) and deceptively eternal *relative to our perspective*. (Here, *experience* is not in quotes as we experience it before death, unlike any nothingness.)

Hypothesis 1 has been accepted as the materialistic orthodoxy by many, despite lacking empirical verification. It's only unaccepted by those who believe in a supernatural kind of consciousness that emerges upon death. Nonetheless, as is true of any such supernational consciousness, Hypothesis 1 can only be verified *after* death, which is impossible.

In contrast, Hypothesis 2 has hitherto been overlooked. Likely, this is because of the orthodoxy of Hypothesis 1, the afterlife beliefs of the religious and spiritualists, and the difficulty in viewing death strictly from a psychological frame of reference—i.e., from the perspective of only what a dying person can perceive. Nonetheless, Hypothesis 2 can be verified *before* death and is, to a large degree, by many human experiences with waking up from timelessness, as discussed in the previous chapter. In Part II, I thoroughly analyze Hypothesis 2 and promote it to a scientific theory.[5]

But first, in this chapter, I explain in more detail the cognitive science principles that support it. Cognitive science is an interdisciplinary field that is much related to psychology but also related to neuroscience and artificial intelligence. It is devoted to studying the mind and its processes, such as perception, reasoning, memory, etc.

Time Perception

To delve deeper into Hypothesis 2 and better grasp how an eternal consciousness can be natural, one must first understand the concept of time and how we subjectively perceive it.

Einstein posited that time "has no independent existence apart from the order of events by which we measure it" (Barnett 1964 19, 47). Philosophers (e.g., St. Augustine) and physicists besides Einstein have long reflected on and debated the meaning of time (Manning, Cassell, & Cassell 2013; Muller 2016, 17–20; Smolin 2013). Is it real within our universe or only an illusion? The debate, however, is irrelevant here because it is only our *perception* of time that is pertinent to deducing the NEC theory. Philosophy describes this perception of time as "changes or events *in* time" and our perceptions of "their temporal relations" (Le Poidevin 2015).

---

[5] I point out in Chapter 8 that in some scientific contexts such promotion is meaningful.

Examples of events that may contribute to one's perception of time or sense of time are the tick of a clock, the flap of a butterfly wing, the blink of an eye, the slightest detectable movement of a thrown ball, a spoken syllable, and the unspoken syllable within the progression of one's train of thought. Perceived events happen when we are awake (alert, imagining, or hallucinating), dreaming, or having an NDE. Our experiences are made up of a stream of events. Perceived events are made up of a stream of conscious static moments.

We continually transition back and forth between perceiving time and not perceiving time. When we do not perceive time, we are simply not perceiving any events and thus no next moment until we again transition back to perceiving time, if indeed we ever do. We begin by transitioning from one eventless and thus timeless state of mind, our before-life, and we end by transitioning into another, our after-life (once again, meaning the period after death).

The dependency of time perception on events implies that when we cannot perceive events within a state of mind (e.g., dreamless sleep), we encounter timelessness. We do not *experience* nothingness as such an "experience" would require more than a conscious moment. Thus, it would take time and necessarily include self—itself, a thing that negates no*thing*ness. So within a state of timelessness, we lose our sense of time, but we do not lose one crucial thing: our sense of self.

To be clear, in a timeless state of mind, we lose our sense of self from the perspective of others (i.e., in their reality). However, *in our mind* (i.e., psychologically), *we* never lose our sense of self. It was present in the last event perceived before entering the timeless state, nothing happens in the timeless state to make us lose it, and so, it becomes timeless until another event is perceived. We never wake up thinking, "Who am I?" and then have to search our memory to figure it out. (The rare exception is if we would wake up to a new present moment—*thereby replacing our last one, which included our sense of self*—and due to dissociative amnesia (Cleveland Clinic 2020), we are temporarily unsuccessful in searching our memory for some self-awareness.)

Time perception became one of the major subfields of psychology as it emerged in the late 1800s (Block & Hancock 2019). It is now also a field within cognitive neuroscience. Survey articles in the field, like Block and Hancock's, and internet searches by me revealed much relevant literature on the subjective perception of time—i.e., *psychological time*—within periods of real time, but none on transitions to and from periods of time imperceptibility—i.e., periods of *psychological timelessness* (Stroud 1955)—as, for example, encountered during dreamless sleep. Perhaps the lack of attention to these transitions should not be surprising given that so many definitions of the field resemble that which I found in a psychology textbook study guide:

> **Time perception** is a field of study within psychology and neuroscience that refers to one's subjective experience of time, which is measured by one's own perception of the duration of the indefinite and continuous unfolding of events. (Cram101 Textbook Reviews 2017, 206)

The lack of attention to these transitions *should* be surprising, though, for in reality, as indicated before, we constantly alternate between psychological time and psychological timelessness. Moreover, we spend roughly a quarter to a third of real time in the latter. Actually, our minds spend almost all of real time in the latter—i.e., in a timeless state wherein time is imperceptible if we view our lives in the context of eternity. Such a view includes our after-life.

Not to think the last statement absurd, perhaps as well as the idea of a *natural* eternal consciousness, one must know that I assume the after-life is, when not explicitly stated otherwise, devoid of any supernatural consciousness. Also, one must understand the cognitive sameness of the transitions into timeless states of mind and of the timelessness of the timeless states no matter the transition type. These types include awake to dreamless sleep, dreaming to dreamless sleep, awake to passed out, and yes, even dying to dead. Moreover, one must understand the psychological and thus relativistic nature of these transitions and the timelessness—i.e., relatively speaking, "It's all in the mind!"

To this end, Figure 4.1 introduces a notation similar to that used in the lifetime-in-eternity model presented in Chapter 7. Like Chapter 7, you can skip the discussion of this figure in the remainder of this section if desired.

Figure 4.1(a) shows the scenario upon which the time-perception field of psychology seems to focus. An individual subjectively perceives a duration of real time between some time t_a and some later time t_b in terms of some sequence of perceived events e_1 through e_j. Of interest are what factors influence psychological time and to what extent.

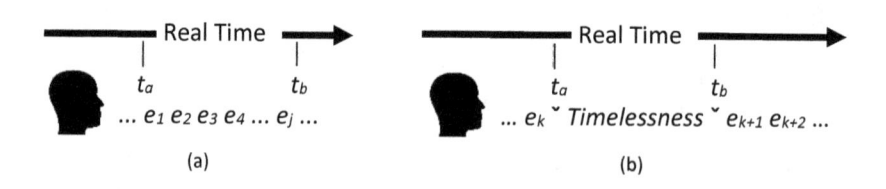

Figure 4.1. Two scenarios relevant to time perception. In an individual's mind, a period of real time between time t_a and time t_b is in (a) subjectively perceived as a sequence of perceived events e_1 e_2 ... e_j and in (b) imperceptible, resulting in *Timelessness* because no events are perceived, including the transitioning events (˘s) into and out of the timelessness.

Figure 4.1(b) shows the scenario relevant to this article. A duration of real time begins at some time t_a when an imperceptible event occurs (denoted by ˘; e.g., fall asleep) that transitions the mind from a time-perceiving state into a timeless state. The last event perceived, which may have been interrupted at some moment, is some event e_k. After this event, no more events are perceived, which results in psychological *Timelessness*. Until at some time t_b, another imperceptible event occurs (denoted by another ˇ; e.g., wake up) that ends the timeless period. This event transitions the mind back into a time-perceiving state wherein some initial event e_{k+1} (e.g., an alarm beep) is immediately perceived, which signals a new conscious awareness.

I stated in the above paragraph that an "*imperceptible* event occurs ... that transitions the mind from a time-perceiving state into a timeless state." Chapter 8 establishes the cognitive principle that all events that transition one into a timeless state (e.g., falling asleep) are never perceived.

Note in (b) that when the imperceptible event at t_a is death, the after-life begins, the event at t_b does not occur, and the events e_{k+1} e_{k+2} ... are not perceived. Also, note that when the event at t_b is birth (or near birth), the before-life ends, the events ... e_k are not perceived, and the event at t_a does not occur.

Conscious Perception

To see the NEC as natural, one must understand not only time perception but conscious perception. Conscious perception relates to how we are aware of our self, environment, activities, sensations, thoughts, feelings, and emotions. The epigraph that begins this chapter states a truth, which is at the root of the NEC. I start to explain it in detail in this section. In Chapter 8, I go the extra mile in establishing that even "to be conscious of" going into and out of "being unconscious" is impossible.

As early as the third century B.C., the Abhidharma Buddhist school posited perception as occurring only in discrete conscious moments, called *dharmas* (Ronkin 2014). According to Herzog et al. (2016), this viewpoint was first reflected in Western science when von Baer (1862) "coined the term 'moment' as the border between the past and the future." Reflecting current science, Herzog et al. state the following:

> We experience the world as a seamless stream of percepts. However, intriguing illusions and recent experiments suggest that the world is not continuously translated into conscious perception. Instead, perception seems to operate in a discrete manner, just like movies appear continuous although they consist of discrete images. (Herzog et al. 2016, Abstract)

Cognitive research (e.g., Elliott & Giersch 2016; Herzog et al. 2016) indicates a sensory "seamless stream of percepts" is processed unconsciously and rendered into a new discrete conscious moment—also referred to as a "psychological moment," "time slice," or "snapshot"—roughly twenty to twenty-five times a second. This rendering not only processes input from our sensory "devices" (eyes, ears, nose, tongue, and skin) but often—and sometimes only, as in dreams—from our stored memories. Each moment is static, just like a frame within a film. That is, it never changes in content but only gets replaced by the next. Consciousness is thus produced as a stream of conscious moments. Such moments make up perceived events.

Imagine a science-fictional selfie. It would capture not only a visual of you and your surroundings but *all* of your sensuous perceptions (e.g., sound or even odor) as well as your sense of self, point of view, occurrent beliefs, emotions, etc. It is capturing a present conscious moment, one's consciousness at a point in time and thus an experience frozen in time.

Thus, in any time-perceiving state of mind, like awake and alert or even dreaming, we consciously perceive events in discrete conscious moments (Herzog et al. 2016; Stroud 1955; von Baer

1862). We perceive, and can thus be cognizant (or aware) of, only one of these moments at a time, the *present* moment, which remains the present one until replaced by the next moment. The present moment includes our sense of self, the flow of time, and life in general by incorporating selective memories from *past* conscious moments and the anticipation of *future* ones—especially the next one, which we naturally anticipate will be consistent with the last. Yet we never really know in the present moment whether the next one will occur.

My claim that each present moment includes a sense of the "flow of time" needs to be squared with my earlier statement that "within a state of timelessness, we lose our sense of time." By the latter, I mean that we lose our perception of the *passage* of time. However, our sense of the flow of time remains. It comes from our memory of past moments that help form the present moment and our inherent anticipation of the next moment. When we see an arrow flying to its target, it is at rest in one location within each moment (i.e., instant). In the next moment, it's at rest in another location. Since within each moment, we carry the memory of its last location and anticipate the next, we perceive the arrow is in motion. This sense of motion corresponds to our sense of the flow of time, so no wonder the phrase "the arrow of time." By the way, if we had no memory (which some creatures do not), we would have no sense of the passage of time (Lanza & Pavšič 2020) and no sense of the flow of time within our final discrete moment.

To summarize, three fundamental aspects of discrete conscious moments deserve emphasis.

1. *Each moment embodies all of the sensations, feelings, and emotions present in an experience at a point in time, many of which have been formed by and carried over from preceding moments. Always present is the feeling—i.e., the "anticipation" as stated above—that more moments will follow that are consistent with the present one.* This aspect is true even when

you expect to fall asleep or die soon. You may know sleep or death will quickly come, but you never expect it to be in the next tiny fraction of a second.

2. *You are aware of only what you perceive in these moments.* How could it be otherwise?

3. *Our awareness in these moments includes self-awareness—i.e., an awareness of self and our awareness.* Given the unknowns, complexities, and differing views on consciousness and definitions of self-awareness, I am tempted to say no more here. However, I will at least state what I mean here by self-awareness. It is knowing who you are (e.g., your personality) and not only being able to experience (e.g., a sunset on the beach) but knowing *what* you are experiencing and that *you* are indeed experiencing it. As I will make clear in the next chapter, computers lack such self-awareness.

Chapter 5

The NEC
Grasping Its Elusive Essence

Any fool can know. The point is to understand.
—Albert Einstein

Simply knowing an NEC exists isn't enough; one must fully understand its precise essence. Analyzing the evidence for the NEC—the relevant human experiences and underlying cognitive science principles—and developing an appreciation of the major role consciousness plays in our view of reality were necessary for me to grasp and precisely describe the essence of the NEC. As discussed in Chapter 2, this was an evolutionary process. And admittedly, in my past articles and comments, I didn't always "get it right," especially in precisely describing the NEC's essence.

Its essence is its core properties. Three of these properties—relativistic, timeless, and eternal—are elusive, and their interplay makes the NEC's essence challenging to explain and grasp. After all, this interplay makes the NEC illusionary from the perspective of the living. As illusionary, which can be seen as a fourth core property, the NEC is as hard to explain in one respect as trying to explain the illusion of a rainbow to a person who has been blind from birth. For then, like the NEC, the rainbow can't be illustrated on paper and its likeness viewed; rather, it can only be imagined.

Before delving into the core properties, I use Figure 5.1 to review NEC theory concepts. It shows a person's final experience (here, an NDE), death, and after-life in real time. The NDE is broken into activities (*as*), the last activity is broken into events (*es*), and the last event is broken into conscious moments (*ms*). The NDE begins (denoted by ˇ) after a period of *Timelessness* and ends (denoted by ˇ) after its final moment. A ˇ represents an imperceptible event that transitions into or from a state of timelessness. The NDE ended naturally or ended because a deteriorating brain could not produce another NDE moment. A period of *Timelessness* precedes the imperceptible event **death** (denoted by the last ˇ). The NEC, here a natural afterlife, begins with the last moment. The etna starts with the first NDE activity. The NEC,

```
                    ──── Real Time ────▶
   ...Timelessness ˇ aaaaaa...eeeee...mmm...m ˇ Timelessness ˇ After-life
                   ├──── final experience ───▶┤
                                         ├──── NEC ────▶
                                         ├── natural afterlife ──▶
                   ├─────────── etna ──────────▶
                 begin                    end           death
                 NDE                      NDE
```

ˇ – imperceptible event
a – activity
e – perceived event
m – conscious moment

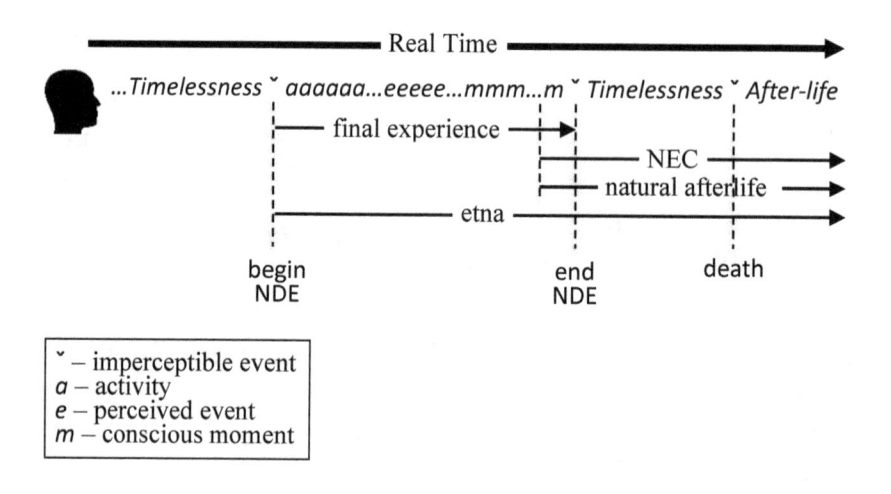

Figure 5.1 The relationships in real time among the concepts associated with the NEC theory: one's final experience (here an NDE); its activities, events, and moments; the NEC, here assumed a natural afterlife; and the etna.

natural afterlife, and etna continue eternally—*but*, unlike real time, only in the mind of the dying person—and timelessly, but only in the minds of the living.

The notation used in Figure 5.1 to represent perceived events, moments, and imperceptible events is like that used in the NEC notation of the lifetime-in-eternity model. As such, it gives you a taste of this notation, which is presented in Chapter 7.

Relativistic, Timeless, Eternal, and Illusionary

Relativity teaches us the connection between the different descriptions [i.e., perspectives] of one and the same reality.
—Albert Einstein

The relativistic essence of the NEC cannot be overemphasized. Its properties must be seen from the proper perspective (i.e., frame of reference). Einstein's special theory of relativity asserts that time is relative to an observer's frame of reference, whether stationary or in motion. The NEC theory asserts that time is also relative to an observer's frame of reference, whether living or dead.

In life, one observes time as a marching parade of events, interrupted by bouts of timelessness, that eventually ends with death. In death, one observes time as only a timeless moment wherein another is anticipated. However, in death from one's frame of reference, one does not perceive this moment as static and thus timeless. Instead, they experience an illusionary sense of time. From the frame of reference of the living, however, the moment, being static, is indeed timeless and constitutes the dying person's NEC.

The NEC is eternal, but only from the frame of reference of the dying person as another moment will never replace their final moment as their present moment. Though eternal to them, they will never be bored with it. Though forever paused in the moment, they always anticipate another, never knowing there will be none. From the frame of reference of the living person, however, the NEC is not eternal because they know that the final moment is materially erased with death and that there'll be no more to come.

Seemingly, humans have always focused on the possibility of a time-perceiving, eternal consciousness that everyone perceives as such—the dead and the living, if the latter could just peer beyond death. Therefore hidden from view has been a relativistic consciousness that is timeless, but *only to the living*, and eternal, but *only to the dead*. Lose sight of the NEC's relativity, and you lose sight of the NEC.

The NEC's not merely eternal, but *timelessly eternal* essence cannot be emphasized enough. Death is an event only perceived by the living, so at death, one is unknowingly and eternally left in a timeless state—i.e., $\Delta t = 0$ (delta *t*, meaning change in real time, equals zero). Memory loss is irrelevant because memory is only necessary when time elapses—i.e., when $\Delta t > 0$. With the NEC, nothing needs to be remembered over time or sustained. Zero energy is required.

The essence of the etna is that it is an eta—i.e., an eventually timeless afterlife—that is natural. An eta is an afterlife that begins as a time-perceiving one but eventually ends as a timeless one (from the perspective of the living). In Chapter 6, I argue that an eta is the only kind of afterlife that can provide the utmost happiness. An eta could be a supernatural kind of afterlife that begins after death. The etna, however, is a natural one because it starts before death as one's last experience, which is perceived as an afterlife, and concludes as an NEC.

As can be seen, to grasp the NEC, its three elusive properties must all be juggled at once: 1) relativistic (i.e., seen differently from different perspectives), 2) imperceptibly timeless, and 3) deceptively eternal. They can sometimes "make your head spin." Table 5.1 summarizes the relationships between these properties.

Table 5.1. Different Perspectives on the NEC

Property	Frame of Reference	
Relativistic	The Dying (Psychological)	The Living (Material)
Timeless	No. *Imperceptibly* paused in their last static moment.	Yes. The last moment is static, thus unchanging.
Eternal	Yes. *Deceptively* so. Left always anticipating another moment.	No. The last moment is erased with death.

The imperception and deception occurring within the dying person's mind make the NEC an illusion, an end-of-life illusion of immortality. Though it's timeless, the experience that leads up to it and instinctive anticipation make it seem time-perceiving to the dying person. Indeed, if they perceive the experience as an afterlife, the etna can be like the afterlife they've always envisioned.

Timely Produced and Timewise Distorted

No matter how tragic and sudden a death—e.g., one is blown apart in a blast—a natural afterlife may still be possible. Research on rats has shown a surge in brain activity for up to thirty seconds after their heart stops beating and blood flow to their brain ends, which is considered *clinical death*. Borjigin et al. (2013) interpret such activity as possible scientific evidence of NDEs. But in humans, is even one second of brain activity needed for the NDE? In an NDE (or a dream), our brain can likely paint a complex heavenly scene almost instantaneously. Also, if an NDE can make "one's life flash before their eyes" (Moddy 2001) in a life review, as has been reported by many NDErs, perhaps in shutting down, our brain can produce an NEC in nanoseconds (i.e., billionths of a second).

Indeed, given the incredible processing speed of the human brain, an NDE seemingly could be produced with such speed. Though the computer has an advantage over the brain in the rate at which it processes basic operations, the brain gains by far the upper hand due to its massively parallel processing (processing many basic operations at once) via its extensive neuron connectivity. It also gains an advantage by its use of analog (i.e., continuous) versus discrete signaling and its reconfiguration of neuron connections with repetitive training (i.e., practice) (Luo 2018). In 2015 a research project at the University of California Berkeley and Carnegie Mellon University estimated that the brain was thirty times faster than the fastest supercomputer (Hsu 2015). However, I'm sure this estimate would be lower today.

It would be interesting to know the rate at which the brain produces NDE and dream moments, given that their production is unencumbered by having to receive and process information from the sensory organs. Seeking this knowledge could be the focus of a future neuroscience research project.

Such research would be especially interesting given the time distortion often occurring within dreams and NDEs. Research has shown that NDErs sometimes feel their NDEs had lasted hours or even days when the actual time could have been no more than seconds or minutes (King 2021a; King 2021b, Green 1968). Human experience with dreams also evidences such distortion in time. To my knowledge, most research in the field of time perception has focused solely on subjects that are awake.

Time distortion plays a significant role in one's end-of-life illusion of immortality and possible etna. With the NEC, time is deceptively eternal. It's deceptive in that the NEC is imperceptibly timeless. Also, as indicated above, the actual time that passes within the preceding time-perceiving experience can be much less than that perceived by the experiencer. In the end, however, what is important is not the real time of the final experience but what is real to the dying person.

An Illusion, Yet Very Real to the Dying Person

While the NEC is an illusion, it is real to the dying person. And its reality can be argued on several fronts. So much so that perhaps it might even be accepted by the living.

First, while the living may not accept that an ELVD or NDE represents reality, they cannot argue that the feelings and emotions aroused by them are not real. They're the same as the fear or relief one experiences when waking up from a nightmare or the love and pleasure one feels when waking up from being with a deceased loved one in a delightful dream. Our feelings and emotions distinguish us from most lesser creatures, so perhaps it shouldn't be surprising if they play a dominant role in our natural afterlife or merely our NEC. They will dominate as the events of your last experience will always be in the past, and there'll be no more in the future. But *you will always be left with feelings and emotions that the experience has aroused, forever*—be they the peace and love, turmoil, or the fear present in that last conscious moment.

Second, NDEs have been described as "even more real than real"—a phrase used to describe the NDE by neurologist Steven Laureys based on studying the NDE memories of coma survivors (Brumfield 2013; Thonnard et al. 2013). Elaborating, Laureys states, "To our surprise, NDEs were much richer than any imagined event or any real event of these coma survivors. The difference was so vast." Thus in a heavenly natural afterlife, one most likely believes it is real and experiences its bliss. Believing now that it's delusional and hence undesirable, as some may (e.g., philosopher P3 whom you will meet in Chapter 11), likely won't change this, making such belief irrelevant. Besides, if the natural afterlife were *real*, how would one experiencing it know that it's real and not just an etna?

Third, in the NEC, one is in the same situation they've been in billions of times. They're in a present moment and aware of their experience, remembering the most recent past events and fully expecting a consistent moment to follow. They may only be "living in the moment" or thinking of the future. For some, this future may be of imminent death, but for others, it may be "an eternity of joyful experiences," as described in Chapter 3. Regardless, the situation is real. They just don't know there won't be another conscious moment.

Finally, how can a phenomenon, a state of mind that has evolved by nature and is produced by nature, not be considered real, i.e., natural? Whether the NEC's content is influenced by a God or even fabricated by humans (via a drug-induced hallucination) is irrelevant.

But What Is Reality?

> *Wherever the life is, [the universe] bursts into appearance around it.*
> —Ralph Waldo Emerson

> *Everything we call real is made of things that cannot be regarded as real.*
> —Niels Bohr, Nobel Prize-Winning Physicist

> *The very study of the external world [leads] to the conclusion that the content of consciousness is an ultimate reality.*
> —Eugene Wigner, Nobel Prize-Winning Physicist

What exactly do we mean by real—i.e., reality? And what is a "real afterlife" anyway? A narrow definition of *reality* relates it to earth-bound, materialistic, and awake and alert experiences. No envisioned afterlife that I am aware of, except reincarnation, is real in this sense. Can the conventional, time-perceiving, perfect-world afterlife be truly real if it's illogical? A broader definition of *reality* would include hallucinations, dreams, and NDEs because they are real life experiences, as noted above. Besides, is reality ever an *actual* reality, or is it always what we perceive as reality?

Figure 5.2 is a picture of the person on the cover of this book looking at a beach sunset. It was taken by an imaginary "ER+HSR Camera"—one of science fiction, like the selfie in the previous chapter. It is positioned and directed as described in the caption. ER stands for *External Reality*. HSR stands for *Human Sensory Reality*. The camera captures the visual part (i.e., an image) of these two kinds of reality. External reality is reality unfiltered and unconstructed via any kind of sensory organ or consciousness. Human sensory reality is that which results from human filtering and construction. It only exists in and is experienced in a human mind and is what Lanza (2009) calls a physical reality.

To be more specific, external reality is what's "'out there' beyond our brains," as I stated before—i.e., our natural world. It's comprised of electromagnetic waves, probability waves or wave functions, and elementary particles or various kinds of quantum fields depending on one's adopted physics model for matter and energy. All of these have no visual properties (i.e., no color). Some do not even materialize as "particles" until they "collapse" based on some probability function when they are measured or "observed" (Brooks 2010; Lanza 2009, 61–81; Muller 2016, 193–230; Quantum 2019). As such, this "reality" isn't even actual as yet, only possible. The white in the picture only *represents* an "image" of external reality, but this reality is not white at all. Absent of any consciousness, it's invisible and thus not an image that can be shown on paper. That's why there's almost nothing in this picture.

The human brain image of this external reality—here, just the visual part of HSR—is captured by the camera only when present and only where it resides. And it resides only within the physical confines of a conscious human brain. The person on the cover is the only person on the beach within the camera's focus; otherwise, there would be more human brain images in the picture.

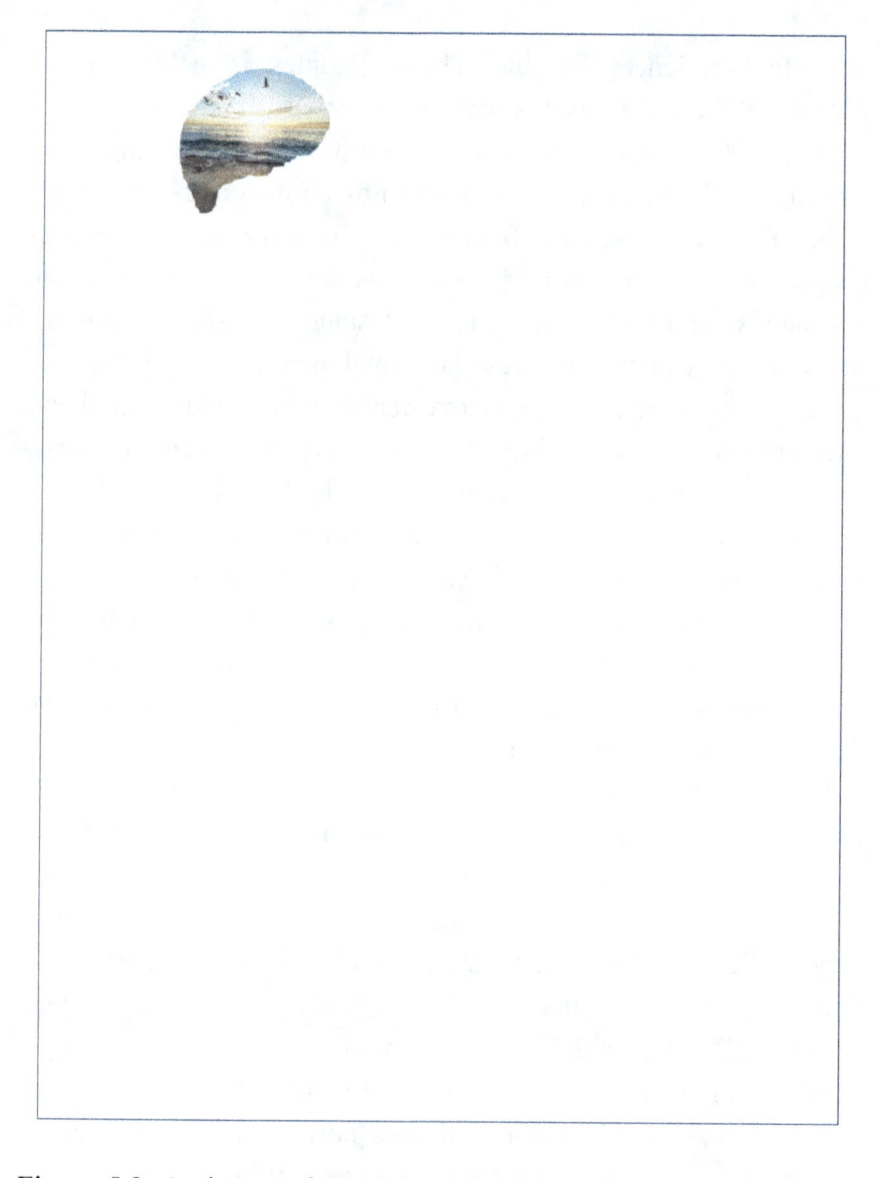

Figure 5.2. A picture of the right side of the same person shown on this book's cover looking directly at a beach sunset. It was taken by a special camera, an "ER + HSR Camera," where ER stands for External Reality and HSR stands for Human Sensory Reality. The camera tripod was placed just to the person's right and aimed along the beach to their left. (Sunset photo by Frank Mckenna on Unsplash.com)

The person's body, besides their brain, is not part of the picture. For it to appear in the picture (in one's mind), someone else must be within the camera's focus and looking at it. Note that if we had an SSR (Seagull Sensory Reality) version of the camera and if the seagulls were close enough and in focus, the reality of the beach scene might look a whole lot different in their minds.

The matter and energy that comprise external reality not only have no visual properties but also have no sound, odor, tactile (i.e., feel), or taste properties. As part of our consciousness, the mind must create what we perceive as physical realities from the input received from our sensory organs. If an ocean wave crashes on the beach and there is no human around, does it make a sound? The answer is no. But if a seagull is around? I will let you research that, but I would think a seagull would hear the waves crashing, but it could be different from what we hear.

Our brain and sensory organs don't allow us to perceive all of what's "out there" in external reality. From what's there, a dog's nose and mind can create and smell odors imperceptible to humans. A bird's sense of subtle variations in the earth's magnetic field allows them to follow a precise migration route. How did this sense evolve? What else may be "out there" that we can't perceive? What percentage are we perceiving? Could a consciousness ever evolve (or is there one) that could perceive it all? The answers to these questions are unknown.

One last note about the ER+HSR camera. It is not capturing the sound of waves crashing on the beach, the feel of the evening sea breezes on the skin, or odors that we can perceive (e.g., a salty sea odor). Nor is it capturing another fundamental reality, which is only created in the mind—the person's feelings and emotions. These are associated with and evoked via their awareness of their experience of their reality. To capture these, we would need to integrate into our ER+HSR camera another fictional camera, the one that took the selfie discussed in Chapter 4.

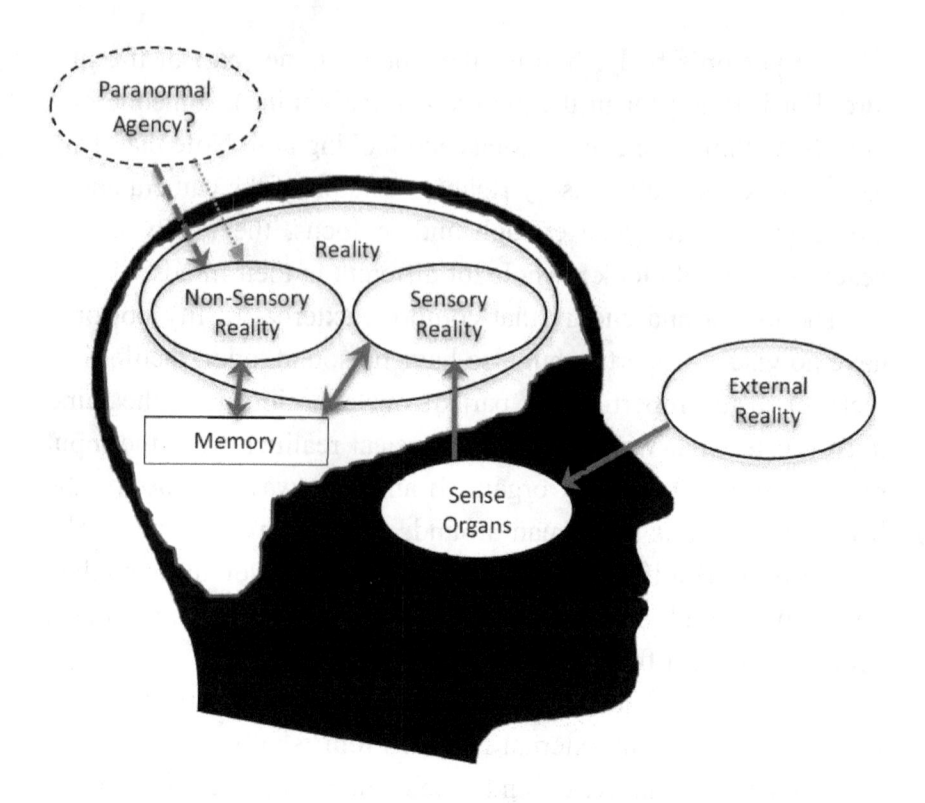

Figure 5.3. A Data Flow Diagram (DFD) that shows the flow of information within a system that produces human reality of two different types. The system includes our brain, our sensory organs, and the external environment, or reality, from which we receive information and upon which we operate. Realities are represented as processes, which are denoted by ovals. Memory is represented as an information store, which is a rectangle. The arrows show the direction of possible information flows. A paranormal agency that possibly influences our non-sensory reality is included as a process in the DFD. Its existence is questionable, as indicated by dashes.

Figure 5.3 presents a data flow diagram (DFD) that may provide a better perspective on reality. A DFD is a systems analysis tool often used in computer science and software engineering. It represents the flow of information among the processes of a system. It is used to accurately describe and so reflect a complete understanding of an existing system and possibly either an enhanced or a new system to replace it.

Here I use it to give more insight into the different realities in a system that includes the human brain, the sensory organs, the natural world in which they exist, and perhaps even some influential paranormal agency. The different realities are represented as ovals since they can be considered processes of consciousness. Processes create, change, and delete objects and exchange information with other processes. They may contain subprocesses. Memory is represented as a rectangle. The location of the ovals and the rectangle in the brain image have nothing to do with the brain areas where processing or storage resides.

As seen in the DFD, our Reality, which essentially is our consciousness, consists of **Sensory Reality** and **Non-Sensory Reality**. **Sensory Reality** is a process that receives information from the **Sense Organs** and **Memory** to form our sensory reality. We experience it when we are awake and alert to our environment. Each of the sense organs—eyes, ears, tongue, skin, and nose—could have been represented by its own oval. The **Sense Organs** are processes that receive information from our **External Reality**—i.e., our external world. The **Sensory Reality** process continually stores information in our memory—e.g., the "look" of our kitchen. This information is then available as input to enhance our **Sensory Reality** or help create our **Non-Sensory Reality**.

Our **Non-Sensory Reality** does not process any information from our **Sense Organs**. We experience it when imagining (e.g., your kitchen), hallucinating, dreaming, or having an NDE. It receives information from our memory and stores information there. This storing (without information as to source) allows us to sometimes remember part of our dreams after waking up but also sometimes question whether we actually experienced something (in our sensory reality) or just dreamt it.

The process **Paranormal Agency** provides input into our **Non-Sensory Reality** and some control over it. The question mark, the dashed oval and output arrow, and the dotted control arrow all indicate the questionable status of this process's existence. Is this agency (or agent) a reality? Some people believe so.

This paranormal agency could be a deity, some universal consciousness, or some of both. Who or what controls our hallucinations, dreams, and NDEs—develops the plot, designs the stage settings, and fabricates the faces of the characters? And does so in nanoseconds? How can some people recall what they experienced on any specific day years ago or recite the digits of *pi* to thousands of decimal places? Is this information stored in their memory, or are they tapping into something most of us cannot access?

The Brain as a Receiver-Filter. The idea that the brain serves as a receiver and filter, tapping into a world of universal consciousness, has been around for some time. As an organ, the brain would then parallel our sensory organs—eyes, ears, nose, and skin—which correspondingly serve to receive and filter input from our material world. An excellent analogy to such a brain would be the smartphone—which receives and filters vast amounts of information from space, existing as radio waves (e.g., television, radio, broadband, or Wi-Fi).

A chapter titled "The Mind Is Not the Brain" in a book by eminent academic psychiatrist Bruce Greyson (2021, 120–130) presents an informative and interesting discussion of the receiver-filter model of the brain and its relationship to NDEs. Greyson speculates that out-of-body experiences (OBEs), which are common in NDEs, could result from a breakdown of the brain's filtering process as it deteriorates near death. Such a breakdown could allow access to the universal consciousness and explain the reports from some NDErs that they could observe their own bodies from above and ongoing rescue or operation activities while being totally unconscious or heavily sedated, respectively (64–76). A speculation on my part is that abnormal brain filtering might also explain how some people with autism exhibit certain mental capabilities well beyond that of most of us. Greyson states that NDEs suggest that the mind, which allows us to experience consciousness, is different from our brains, which actually limit consciousness when functioning normally.[6]

Thought Experiments. Some thought experiments may clarify the distinction between our different realities shown in Figure 5.3. Suppose no one is in your kitchen (i.e., no observer). What's the reality in there? When you're not in there, you probably think that your kitchen is just as it was when you last left it—i.e., as it appears in your sensory reality. But as shocking as it may be, it is not. And not even close!

When you're thinking of your kitchen but not in it, it exists only in your imagination. You are retrieving the image you have of your kitchen from your memory, making it your non-sensory reality. But in reality (i.e., external reality), the kitchen is just like Figure 5.2, minus the image in the brain of the person's sensory reality. And this is true even if all of the kitchen lights are on!

---

[6] Greyson, however, crosses a great divide when he abruptly goes from the idea that the mind is not "totally dependent on the brain" (124), which Figure 5.3 accommodates, to the idea that "our minds are independent of our brains" (123), an idea that to me is, at least now, "a bridge too far." He gets there by assuming there exist "conditions ... when the brain stops working but the mind keeps going" (124), but he gives no sound scientific evidence of such conditions. Figure 5.3 indicates that information (i.e., knowledge) and the insight it brings may come from some paranormal agency along with some control over non-sensory brain processes. Greyson, however, goes much further in positing that "our thoughts and feelings come from outside the body" and that our brain filters "out those that are not essential to our physical survival" (128). Well, if this is true, my brain seems to be doing a poor job of filtering. Ending the chapter, he states that "If our minds can function independently of our brains ... then might it be possible that our minds could continue to function ... after we die?" (129, 130) That's *"continue"!* Not just be *paused* as in the NEC. My answer to the question is, "Sure, but the truth of the key premise has not yet been nearly established."

It is only when you go into your kitchen with eyes open that invisible electromagnetic waves, which are reflected (at 186,282 miles per second) off various types of invisible atoms within the room, enter your eyes. Only those waves, as photons, with frequencies within a very tiny range are detected by your retina's cone or rod cells. The neural circuitry of your eyes and brain then translates their frequencies, locations, directions, and densities within groupings into colors, brightness, and patterns. The colored patterns are then recognized by your brain via stored memories (i.e., knowledge) as three-dimensional objects of different types (e.g., a refrigerator), and, Whalah! Your kitchen emerges.

Now suppose your kitchen is on fire, and you can't put it out. Thankfully, it's only a nightmare. You're experiencing your non-sensory reality.

Summary. Five points should be emphasized about reality:

1. Both our sensory and non-sensory realities are a product of our minds.
2. Both are physical realities, as defined by Lanza, in the sense that the brain is creating a 3-dimensional reality in space-time. In our external reality, there is no 3-dimensional space (as it requires depth perception), no colors or shapes (as they must be seen), no solid surfaces (as they must be felt), no sounds (as they must be heard), and no odors (as they must be smelled).
3. Except for lucid dreams, those in which the dreamer is aware they are dreaming, we perceive no difference between our sensory and non-sensory realities while experiencing them.
4. As Figure 5.2 and the kitchen thought experiment illustrate and as biocentrism emphasizes, "reality is all in the mind." Though I have identified an external reality, there is no reality—i.e., nothing exists—without it being perceived. Consciousness is essential for somethingness. (Ehlmann 2014)
5. Whatever reality is in the mind at death will be paused.

Objections (or Difficulties in Understanding?)

I have seen that four interrelated facets of the NEC, two properties and two cognitive principles on which it relies, make it especially difficult to grasp. All of these must be understood and accepted:

1. Timeless—i.e., it is something that never changes.
2. Relativistic—i.e., its existence depends on one's frame of reference.
3. Reliance on two operative cognitive science principles of human consciousness:
   (a) we are only aware of that which we perceive within discrete conscious moments and
   (b) our awareness includes self-awareness, which is an awareness of self and of our awareness (i.e., meta-awareness).

Below I discuss some objections to the NEC or natural afterlife that have been expressed to me and give my response. They show these four facets being either ignored or misunderstood. I do this because others may have these same objections. I also discuss a false analogy to the NEC specifically related to facet 3(b) above.

In reviewing my NEC theory article (Ehlmann 2020), a journal referee strongly objected to my use of the phrase "timelessly eternal" in the abstract to describe the NEC, stating that it was a contradiction in terms because something *timeless* cannot be *eternal*. I responded:

> Disagree! Both are the proper terms for describing the NEC. From *Merriam-Webster* (MW): **timeless** – 2 :not affected by time :AGELESS. From MW: **eternal** – 1 a :having infinite duration :EVERLASTING. These meanings do not contradict each other.

Having "gotten off on the wrong foot," the referee often misinterpreted and took issue with other descriptions of the NEC. Unfortunately, this referee's confusion and impatience led to a rejection after reading very little of my article.

Another person, commenting on a philosophy forum, objected to the exact phrase. He stated that the notion of something being both timeless and eternal was incoherent. I responded with the same definitions given above and then added:

> The NEC is a moment *not affected by time*—i.e., a discrete moment that never changes—and a moment *having infinite duration*—i.e., it lasts forever from the perspective of the dying person. Think of a photograph, which never changes, printed on material that never decomposes.

When this person still objected, stating that photographs do deteriorate over time and *everything changes*, and challenged me for another example, I responded:

> 1 + 1 = 2 never changes. The truth of a tautology never changes. The laws of nature never change. The fact that something *occurred* never changes and is eternally part of history. The moment *captured* by a selfie never changes.

The latter two examples are analogous to the NEC. For a deceased person, the NEC "occurred" in the mind just before death and was eternally "captured" in their awareness (see principle 3b above).

Most of those who object to the NEC theory do so, and often very readily, because they just cannot seem (or refuse?) to grasp the relativistic nature of the NEC (facet 1). A "Steve" on Quora (https://www.quora.com/) stated:

> ... you'd like us to believe that despite the brain literally not existing anymore (even to the extent of rotting, being cremated ...), our final thought/memory, which is entirely a manifestation of the organ and stored in it, would remain "frozen in time." Where exactly? Consciousness/the mind

is a product of the brain so must go when the physical brain does.

He goes on to argue that if any "Consciousness continues after death," it must continue "somewhere, somehow."

After some back and forth, trying in vain to get Steve "to see the light" related to facets 1 and 2, my final response was:

The NEC requires no physical space (no "somewhere") and no mechanism (no "somehow") operating over time (no "continue")! It is psychological and timeless! You seem incapable of putting yourself in the mind of the dying person and remaining in this frame of reference. Rather, you continue to want to view the NEC from outside their mind, from a material frame of reference. *Yes, from this perspective* [i.e., materially], *the NEC does not exist.*

I have gotten reactions from several philosophers on the NEC theory. Here I discuss the reactions of one of them, a very prominent philosopher (listed in Wikipedia), whom I anonymously refer to as P1. In Chapter 11, I discuss the reactions of two more. P1 argued that once the brain is dead, there will be no energy to sustain a dream or NDE, especially a never-ending one.

P1 expressed to me that a "subjectively endless dream" occurring in a "finite interval" of time would require a brain (i.e., a physical system) to "process an infinite amount of information." This, he stated, would be thermodynamically impossible. My response was:

With the NEC, no "subjectively endless dream" occurs in a "finite interval of real time." The dream occurs in such an interval, but it does not "process an infinite quantity of information" because with death, it's over, done! It is endless, subjectively so, only from the illusionary perspective of the dying person, and it *is timeless*—i.e., $\Delta t = 0$, meaning the change in time is zero, no interval! Thus, no energy is required to sustain it, and the laws of thermodynamics do not apply.

Others have argued that once the brain is dead, there will be no memory of the last experience. A comment to me, once posted in Quora (https://www.quora.com/) but then apparently deleted, reads:

> Your assumption is that they have some level of awareness after they die, something for which we have no evidence. Some level of awareness is required for them to have any ongoing memory of the last thing they experienced. Where is your evidence that this is the case?

Here the person is not grasping any of the NEC facets listed above, which are all interrelated. My response is given below, wherein I quote from the above and give the relevant facet number in brackets.

> I certainly *do not* assume "they have some level of awareness after they die." They don't. They do in their last moment before death but then are consciously left in that moment only to *deceptively* "believe" (are aware) [3b] they do (when they do not). They never are aware their last experience has ended, and if they are not aware that it has, then *to them* [2], it never will [3a]. Get it? Once dead, they don't "have any ongoing memory of the last thing they experienced." But they don't need it because the NEC is timeless ($\Delta t = 0$) [1]. A memory is required only when there's a passage of time ($\Delta t > 0$) between a moment experienced and the need to recall it, which is not the case in the NEC relative to the dying, then dead, person [2].

Some who've commented on the NED theory have tried to refute it via analogy. They likened the human mind to a computer and claimed that, like the computer, once the mind "loses power," it loses all function and, therefore, all consciousness. This, however, is a false analogy in that a computer is not like a human in two very relevant aspects.

First, it lacks self-awareness (i.e., facet 3b). It has no awareness (i.e., knowledge) of its self and of that which it is aware or "conscious,"—i.e., of its current state. For example, if a computer is generating the tenth digit of π, just as we might be doing by hand, it does not *know* it is doing such as we would know. It never thinks to itself (or believes), "I'm now generating the tenth digit of pi." Thus, with the loss of power, it's not left with the illusionary knowledge (i.e., belief) that it's still experiencing its final state (e.g., generating that tenth digit) like a dying person is left with the belief that they're still experiencing their last conscious moment and thus experience.

Second, a computer lacks the feelings and emotions (e.g., pain and love, respectively) that are present in human consciousness and arise from self-awareness. It never feels good about its accomplishments or loves what it is doing. The self-awareness part of our consciousness is paramount in creating the NEC.

For those interested in a valid computer analogy, I give one below. However, it relies on creating a fictitious computer, enhanced with a more humanlike "consciousness." For those not interested, you may skip to the last paragraph of this section.

> Like real computers, when my computer is on ("alive"), even in sleep mode, all data relevant to its current processing task ("experience") is stored in registers and main ("short-term") memory. The content of this data after any revision is its present task status and corresponds to *part of* the computer's present "discrete conscious moment." My enhancement stores data corresponding to the other part of this "conscious moment" in special registers within the core of the processing unit. The content of this data *somehow* "psychologically" gives my computer a "present self-

awareness" about itself, what task it is executing, the present status of the task, and its related feelings and emotions. Such "present awareness" can never be erased but only changed by a new "conscious moment."

Now, when the computer crashes ("dies"), never to be rebooted ("live") again, its function and thus its last processing task ("experience") ends, and no new "conscious moment" will ever replace the last one. Moreover, just like real computers, my computer will never be aware that it crashed and that there'll be no new "conscious moment." Thus, its "present awareness" will, *from its perspective,* be timelessly eternal, even if it is completely smashed!

I've given this fictitious computer what nature (or a God) has given us as part of our consciousness but what we do not yet know how to give to our computers. That is why I can only state "somehow" above in regard to how I bestowed self-awareness.

Those not interested in how the NEC theory relates to what philosophy teaches about death and immortality can skip to the next chapter.

For Philosophy, A New Type of Immortality

To begin to understand how the NEC theory relates to what philosophy currently teaches about death, immortality, and the afterlife, one could sit in on a philosophy class lecture on these matters. I was able to do just that before writing this section. The lecture was titled "Death and Immortality" and was part of an introductory online philosophy class with the course title "God, Faith, and Reason." The University of Utah offered the class, and as of this writing, it is available on Academia.edu (Barrientos & Petrozzo 2021). Teaching assistant and four-year philosophy PhD candidate Alex Barrientos impartially and expertly taught it, with helpful questions and commentary supplied by Graduate Fellow Katie Petrozzo. I venture that the material presented in this lecture is not much different from that taught in many philosophy of religion courses.

To indicate the impact that I think the NEC will have on philosophy, I now briefly review relevant material presented in the lecture in light of the NEC. Being confident in the NEC's validity, I must admit that while listening, I couldn't help but think, "if only they knew," the "they" meaning the instructor and students as well as the renowned philosophers being discussed.

The fields of philosophy most impacted by the NEC are the philosophy of religion and the philosophy of mind. Both are concerned with whether or not there's a soul and, if so, its connection with the body. The former field studies religions and delves into whether there's a God or an afterlife, God's nature, and the role of the body and soul in any afterlife. The latter field studies the nature of the mind and its relation to the physical world and the body. It delves into the meaning of identity—i.e., what defines an individual, a self, and perhaps a soul.

One of the first slides in the lecture addresses the meaning of immortality (4:10). It first lists two restrictions for its manifestation. The first is "Survival of the individual person, with their character, memories, etc. intact," and the second is "Conscious awareness of that person that they've survived death." To me, these restrictions are too severe. Must all memories remain intact? Requiring such implies the ability to recall these memories. I can see why recalling bad memories might be important in purgatory or Hell, but "why in Heaven"? If one must retain bad memories, won't this make Heaven, any heaven, less than perfect? Also, do we really expect our character to remain the same if we make it into Heaven? We should hope for better for ourselves and others; otherwise, Heaven would be less than perfect.

Regarding the second restriction, the instructor states that without the awareness of one's death, immortality "wouldn't really be important or worthwhile" (5:20). But why, if you're extremely happy in an afterlife, perhaps you're in Heaven, do you need to be aware of your death? Being aware of and able to recall the circumstances of one's death, especially if unpleasant, may not make for the utmost happiness in one's afterlife. Ironically, the immortality of Heaven, as described in the Bible's New Testament, may not meet this condition. Jesus states, "Truly, truly, I say to you, if any one keeps my word, he will never see death" (RSV, John 8:51). If you never see death, must you still somehow be made aware of it?

After the slide states these restrictions, it defines immortality as "A conscious state in which the individual continues to exist after death" (7:20). I believe this simple definition, without any restrictions, expresses the meaning that most people attach to immortality. The restrictions (perhaps added by the more materialist inclined?) may help explain why philosophers never envisioned the NEC. Also, whoever framed these restrictions most likely assumed that any immortality would be time-perceiving and not relativistic. That is, any afterlife would be perceived the same by both the living and the dead if the former could peer into the afterlife and observe the events taking place.

Minus these assumptions, the given definition raises a question. What frame of reference are we talking about here? Does "continues to exist" mean from the material perspective of the living or from the psychological perspective of the dying person? With the NEC, of course, it's the latter and, I think most people would agree, the most important—perhaps even the only one that counts.

The lecture then focuses on three main views of immortality that are said to exist, at least within the western philosophical tradition. These are the materialist view, which denies an afterlife; the dualist view, which affirms an afterlife; and the holistic view, which also affirms an afterlife (10:30).

The materialist view is that mind and body are coexistent so that when the body dies, the brain and thus the mind goes with it (11:30). It rejects the existence of a soul or spiritual self that can survive outside the body. This view was advocated by the ancient Greek philosophers Democritus, Leucippus, and Epicurus as well as Roman philosopher and poet Lucretius. It was seen as therapeutic by the latter two because it eliminates any fear of death. The materialist view is the predominant view among today's academic philosophers (1:26:00, 1:34:36).

The dualist view, also called the Platonic view, is that the mind (psyche, self, or soul) is separate from the body and that when the body dies, the soul lives on (13:50). Death is seen as the liberation of our spiritual being, our essential part, from our short-term bodies. In ancient Greece, this view was held by Pythagoras and further developed by Plato. In modern philosophy, it was promoted by French philosopher René Descartes (1596–1650), who gave us the axiom "I think, therefore I am."

The holistic view is that the soul is not liberated from the body at death but that a new glorified version of the body emerges at some point (16:20). Here, the person is seen as holistic in that the soul is the spiritual manifestation of a material body. Christians, Jews, and Muslims generally hold the holistic view but with a mixture of opinions on two questions. When does the glorified body come into being, and where's the disembodied soul in the meantime? Christianity and Islam teach that the soul enters into an intermediate state at death and is joined with a glorified body on resurrection day. However, early Christian doctrine was heavily influenced by the Platonic view, which is still held by many Christians today and only differs from the holistic view in that no body ever rejoins the soul (18:25).

Besides these main views on immortality, for historical context, the instructor briefly discusses the ancient Homeric view of death (22:52). Here, only the gods are immortal; however, for a mortal:

> [T]here is still something in the house of Hades, a soul and a phantom but no real life in it at all. (Homer, *The Iliad*)

Some semblance of a person, a mere "shadow," survives death—entering a very dull, though not unpleasant, place.

The NEC theory supports the dualist view; however, immortality isn't what one would expect, and the theory offers some solace to the adherents of the other immortality views. In the NEC, the separation of soul and body is eternal, but only from the psychological perspective of the dying person. It's not eternal from the material perspective of the living. Thus some adherents of the materialist view, until they die, may find refuge in claiming it's not *really* immortality. Also, from the material perspective, the NEC is timeless in that it's just a static moment in the dying person's mind followed only by the timelessness that comes from death. However, from the psychological perspective, it's not timeless because the dying person is unknowingly paused in their last moment expecting another to follow. As I've already mentioned, I believe that the advocates of all of the immortality views have assumed immortality to be time-perceiving and never imagined it to be relativistic—i.e., imperceptibly timeless and deceptively eternal psychologically, and thus illusionary, but merely timeless and momentary materialistically.

As indicated in Chapter 1, the NEC theory does not rule out the possibility that the NEC could be overridden at or sometime after death by some supernatural afterlife. So, for the adherents of the holistic view of immortality, this possibility means that the NEC can be the intermediate state for the soul before eventually uniting with a resurrected, glorified body. I discuss this more in the next chapter and Chapter 11.

Also, the next chapter points out that one's NEC can be numb and dull—essentially near-nothingness. The adherents of the Homeric view, if any remain, may find this to their liking.

THE NEC: GRASPING ITS ELUSIVE ESSENCE

Next, the lecture presents the case given by Plato and his mentor Socrates for the dualist view (22:48), then the argument given by Scottish philosopher David Hume (1711-1776) against the dualist view and immortality in general and for the materialist view (50:40). The instructor emphasizes that Hume's arguments should not be seen as "decisive refutations" of immortality but instead "challenges or considerations against."

One can take issue with many arguments on both sides of the debate. I will point out that one crucial piece of "Empirical evidence against immortality" (1:18:50) that Hume gives in support of his "Mind-Body Materialism" view (1:19:40) ironically supports the contrary view. Hume considers this evidence as his most relevant, and the instructor views his argument, for mind-body inseparability, as "one of his strongest" (1:26:20, 1:33:12). But to me, the fact that the evidence and argument are considered such helps explain why the NEC wasn't discovered earlier. So, what's this piece of evidence?

Hume is wrong in claiming that "Dreamless sleep as a preview of what awaits us when the body dies" is evidence of Mind-Body Materialism. Instead, based on human experience (Chapter 3) and cognitive science principles (Chapter 4) and as is formally deduced in Chapter 8, this "preview" (or foretaste) is evidence of something non-material. This is a paused consciousness with timelessness (PCT), which supports a psychological NEC. Dreamless sleep, like death, is cognitively sheer timelessness. While dreamlessly sleeping, we still believe we're watching a TV show until we wake up, and we still think we're at a party until we wake up and see the party is over and the guests have left. And, while experiencing a heavenly ELDV or NDE, if fortunate enough, we'll still believe we're experiencing our heaven until we wake up. And if we never wake up? Our last conscious moment is a timeless cognitive capsule of our self-awareness of an experience at a point in time, an anticipation of another consistent moment to follow, our feelings and emotions, *and our soul*. Only another conscious moment can erase it as our present moment, but we'll never perceive this moment as we'll never perceive our moment of death.

To close this section, I respond to two more arguments Hume gives. He sees both as more empirical evidence against immortality.

First, he invokes the Doctrine of Flux, which states that everything is constantly changing—i.e., nothing is eternal (1:29:49). Given this, he asks why should only one thing, a human life (or a soul), be immortal. I've encountered and responded to this "everything changes" argument before (see the last section). So again, some non-material things never change—e.g., logic, mathematics, or the laws of physics. (The latter only changes in our efforts to get them right.) More relevant to immortality, a materially produced discrete conscious moment and corresponding immaterial self-awareness never change but can only be replaced.

Second, Hume invokes Aristotle's NDNIV (nature does nothing in vain) argument (1:31:22). He claims that if immortality exists, nature would be wasteful in making humans dread death and work so hard, only in vain, to avoid it. But, if immortality doesn't exist, this dread and avoidance would make more sense. Hume seems to assume that any afterlife will be pleasant, but humans don't believe that. I would add that individuals "working" hard to avoid an unpleasant afterlife benefits them and society (as I explain in Chapter 12) and thus their evolution. Possibly, nature's purpose for immortality? Also, regarding NDNIV, what is nature's purpose for NDEs if not for producing a very intense and all too real NEC-type of immortality?

Chapter 6

The NEC Theory
Understanding Its Momentous Aspects

In this chapter, I finally get around to discussing in more depth some significant aspects of the NEC theory and the phenomena it brings to light, which I have called the NEC, the natural afterlife, and the etna.

Provides a Dreamlike and Spiritual NEC

The NEC is dreamlike when based on a dream, vision, or hallucination (ELDV) or NDE. Both ELDVs and NDEs: provide an alternative, spiritual experience; present a non-sensory reality as defined in Chapter 5; can be very intense and indistinguishable from sensory reality; are mysteriously produced in content; have been historically viewed by many as providing a potential passage into a transcendental realm; and can be perceived as an afterlife. *Merriam-Webster* defines a dream as "a series of thoughts, images, and sensations occurring in a person's mind during sleep" and hallucination as "a sensory perception (such as a visual image or a sound) that occurs in the absence of an actual external stimulus—i.e., external reality."

Some unique features of NDEs, however, should be pointed out. NDEs typically occur in a brain-diminished state, while dreams occur in sleep and visions and hallucinations occur in wakefulness. Other notable differences are 1) the NDE can be even more intense than a dream and so have a more lasting impact (Noyes, Fenwick, & Holden 2009), so much so that many claim their NDE was not dream-like (Long 2003); 2) OBEs (out-of-body experiences) are common in NDEs but not in dreams or visions; and 3) as pointed out in Chapter 3, the NDE can occur while being fully anesthetized, whereas dreams cannot, implying a differing production mechanism (or source). (Greyson, Kelly, & Kelly 2009, p. 226; Hameroff 2010b)

Regarding whether an etna occurs with death, some differences between NDEs and ELDVs may not be that important (but certainly not #3 above). The possibility exists that a dying person has no NDE but instead has an intense ELDV. As indicated in Chapter 1, ELDVs have been recorded throughout history and are very common. The focused study conducted by Kerr et al. (2014 Abstract) and reported on in Hoffman (2016) found that comforting perceptions of meeting deceased loved ones within ELDVs were more prevalent as participants approached death. It seems plausible that some ELDVs have been reported as NDEs and, with death, may also result in etnas.

Whether the etna results from an ELDV or NDE, it is spiritual in that all beings—the NDEr, other humans, and nonhumans—are present only in spirit, certainly not in body. No physical objects and no physical space are involved where physical is defined as that which exists in external reality, as described in Chapter 5. The etna exists beyond external time and space as the conscious mind creates its own time and space—i.e., its own physical reality.

Independent of NDE Explanations

As discussed in Chapter 2, some scientists think that NDEs are purely the creations of brain physiology, perhaps involving similar mechanisms as dreams, while others contest such views. Dr. Kevin Nelson (2011), a neurologist who studies NDEs, thinks NDEs employ the same brain apparatus used for dreaming within a REM (rapid eye movement) state of mind. Also, the OBE, sometimes an initial part of the NDE, is thought by some to be related to lucid dreaming (Green 1995; Levitan & LaBerge 1991; Nelson 2011). However, Greyson, Kelly, & Kelly (2009) provide a credible rationale as to why current physiological "explanatory models" (i.e., explanations) cannot account for some NDE features. They argue that serious consideration should be given to a transcendental explanatory model where "some level of reality transcends the physical world." This level can be seen as the **Paranormal Agency** that I included in Figure 5.3, which may be active in producing our non-sensory reality.

Explanations of how NDEs and OBEs occur are irrelevant to the validity of the NEC theory. Also irrelevant is evidence that similar experiences happen to people when they are not near death.

The things relevant to the NEC theory about NDEs relate to their unique features described in the last section. NDEs provide "thoughts, images, and sensations" very near to death, seemingly nearer than dreams, that can be "even more real than real," seemingly more so than dreams. They can do so despite (or perhaps because of) a brain's deteriorating state and even within a fully anesthetized state. Thus, they provide a final, very intense, perceptive moment of an experience that becomes the NEC with the loss of all subsequent perception. Moreover, they often provide an experience that the NDEr perceives as an afterlife.

Natural and Religiously Neutral

The NEC theory uniquely labels the eternal consciousness it defines as natural because, unlike the other afterlife varieties envisioned, its definition is within the scope of present scientific understanding. As such, it provides religious naturalism with a naturally evolved and produced immortal consciousness and afterlife. Many of its adherents, who find religious meaning only in nature and reject any supernatural realm (Crosby 2002, 4; Stone 2008), will likely find this gift of nature rather shocking.[7]

The NEC theory merely defines the existence of the NEC, implicitly claiming it as the default after-life (note the hyphen again). It does not deny the existence of a supernatural eternal consciousness or afterlife, no matter how apparently illogical or (at least for now) unscientific. Such an eternal consciousness could be an after-death NDE (as some see it) or another afterlife that immediately or later overrides the NEC. This afterlife would provide a new perceived present—e.g., the initial conscious moment of an after-death NDE, judgment day, or reincarnation. But the bottom line is that your NEC is guaranteed to be in effect if a supernatural, faith-based afterlife does not begin at death.

A Wild Variety of NEC and Afterlife Experiences

As stated in Chapter 1, the only two main after-life possibilities that humans have considered for centuries have been a) a nothing-

---

[7] An article by Thomas W. Clark (1995) is telling as to why a religious naturalist may find the *natural* afterlife surprising. Clark comes so near to discovering the NEC, stating: "If I am unconscious for any length of time [,] I don't experience that interval; I am always 'present'; this is personal subjective continuity." and "… the notion of a blank or emptiness following death is incoherent, and that therefore we should not anticipate the end of experience when we die." Yet, rather than stay on a subjective (i.e., psychological) path and see the NEC within view, Clark's naturalism-related materialism bias makes him abruptly veer off. He ends up positing personal nonexistence upon death and *generic subjectivity*—meaning, experience continues with death, but only within a new being.

ness, like that of our before-life, or b) some type of event-filled, supernatural afterlife. The NEC theory provides possibilities *close to* both and a continuum in various personalized, timeless neverending experiences in between—from heavenly to humdrum to hellish.

The NEC theory does not say what the content of an NEC will be. It could be a celestial communion with angels, a glorious day on the beach (as seen on the cover of this book), or an eerie encounter with demons. Whether an NEC is an "afterlife" is subjective. It depends to some extent on its content and intensity and to a large extent on "the eye of the beholder."

This section discusses some possible variations in the NEC experience. The last moment of these final experiences ranges from near-nothingness, which is often the case when you fall asleep at night in the quiet of your bedroom, to an extremely pleasurable, highly sensuous, intensely emotional moment anticipating a joyful eternity knowing that you have gone to heaven. In life, the former moment is almost always erased by one's first awake moment and quickly forgotten. But in death, both it and the latter moment remain the present. The latter moment has been reported by many NDErs (Zingrone & Avarado 2009).

Examples of NEC Experiences. One can grasp the many variations in the NEC experience when one considers the kinds of experiences that often occur before one transitions into temporary timelessness and imagines what one's final moment may be.

First, consider in more detail the ordinary, dull, and emotionless moment that one often experiences just before falling asleep each night with eyes closed, fully expecting to fall asleep at any second. As we lie in bed, this moment embodies our sense of self in all its facets and an awareness of our surroundings, but we may see nothing, hear nothing, smell nothing, taste nothing, and may physically and consciously feel nothing. We may see darkness behind our eyelids if we take notice, differentiating it from self. This moment is not nothingness because we're aware of three things: our self, our surroundings, and perhaps the darkness. Alternatively, our mind is focused on some trivial dispassionate thought so that we do not take notice of the darkness and thus do not perceive it. In either case, when we awake, we do not dwell on our last awake moment, so it is erased from our consciousness. The reason is that the new awake present moment isn't extraordinary because it presents nothing unexpectedly different from that embodied in our last moment, like waking up in another room, and it gets our immediate attention.

If, however, we never wake up and never have a new present moment, this awake and final moment, as described, is our NEC, which can be seen as near-nothingness. This NEC is what people can now view as the blandest type of "dying in your sleep" (assuming no intervening ELDV or NDE).

Obviously, many variations are possible for one's awake and final moment before falling asleep, each providing a different NEC. First, dying *peacefully* in your sleep would be almost like near-nothingness, but, quite significantly, one's final moment (and thus NEC) would include feelings of peace and contentment. Second, one can literally or figuratively "cry oneself to sleep," or third, fall asleep happy and content in someone's loving arms. If one never wakes up from these experiences, one's final moment is the NEC, complete with the associated emotions. Fourth, as in a previous thought experiment (Chapter 3), one's final moment could involve a scene from a movie. Fifth, the final moment could involve being at a party. If we fall asleep at a party and wake up some hours later, we immediately wonder, "Where have all the people gone?" If you never wake up, they will still be there in your NEC.

Consider other awake experiences. First, consider the last moment before one passes out from some traumatic experience, like an accident. Will this perhaps terrifying moment become the NEC?

Or will it, as often occurs after waking up from such an experience, have been graciously replaced via amnesia and a "rewind" (◄◄) of the stream of consciousness to some prior present moment? Second, consider a drug hallucination. Who knows what the final hallucinatory moment will encompass? Third, consider the last moment of a visionary kind of ELDV. As mentioned, such a hallucination may often include deceased loved ones—perhaps a child, a spouse, or even both. Much of what I say below about dreams also applies to hallucinations.

Any final awake moment described above could later be overridden by the dream kind of ELDV. The content and intensity of a dream are usually totally beyond one's control, and the experience and final dream moment they provide can be very realistic, sensuous, and emotional. Although the sensory perceptions and events within dreams are not real in a material sense since they are created from memory or perhaps some paranormal agency (see Chapter 5), they seem very real. Also, the very intense emotions they can invoke are real (McNamara 2014; van der Linden 2011). As discussed in Chapters 3 and 5, they are the same as those we sometimes experience when we wake up from a dream (e.g., pleasure or frustration). These emotions and the whole dream experience that is interrupted by death "live on" in the NEC, and emotions are what may be foremost in the mind and the most momentous.

Any of the final moments described above, including that of a dream experienced just before becoming fully anesthetized, could later be overridden by an NDE. Everything stated above about a dream and its final moment is true about an NDE.

Although the natural afterlife could result from an ELDV, the NDE often delivers what many NDErs view as an afterlife, either heavenly or hellish. Thus it is not surprising that many consider the NDE an after-death experience. Given that an NDE is more likely to be perceived as a natural afterlife than other experiences, it's worthwhile to review some of the characteristics of NDEs given previously and point out others.

More About NDEs. As mentioned in the last section, NDEs can be even more realistic and intense than dreams and, as studies have shown, often have a more lasting impact on the lives of NDErs. Again, so much so that many NDErs claim their NDE was not a dream.

It should be comforting to know that studies have also shown that most NDEs are pleasurable. The most common features of these NDEs (and thus, perhaps etnas) include OBEs; heightened senses; being guided or surrounded by light; otherworldly; one or more feelings of peace, joy, or cosmic unity; and encountering mystical or familiar human beings (Kellehear 2009; Zingrone & Alvarado 2009). Variations, however, abound.

Unfortunately, I must mention what is less comforting to know about NDEs. Variations on NDEs include the *distressing NDE (dNDE)*, a term used by Nancy Evans Bush (2009) to describe a "'frightening,' 'negative,' or 'hellish'" NDE. Based on many NDE studies, she concludes that the percentage of dNDEs among those reported is "possibly in the middle to high teens" but also that likely "dNDEs are underreported" (81). For some, a dNDE includes a life review—which can "flash before their eyes," as mentioned in the previous chapter, and be quite unpleasant.

Variations in NDE content may result from a person's life experiences, beliefs, culture, interpretations of experiences, near-death brain physiology, or some combination. However, research on reported NDEs has shown that none of these factors can reliably predict the content of an NDE (Greyson, Kelly, & Kelly 2009, 226; Holden, Long, & MacLurg 2009).

Whether the NEC is a "deathday" gift from God or nature and whether a paranormal agency (see Chapter 5) plays a role in fashioning it may forever be a matter of one's religious or spiritual faith or lack thereof. (I discuss this topic further in Chapter 11.) The fashioning, however done, permits the NEC to be profoundly personalized. The human beings that often appear in NDEs, who may be deceased or still living, are most often those who were emotionally close to the NDEr (Zingrone & Alvarado 2009).

Regarding the NEC, keep in mind that all NDE research studies are based on a relatively small, misrepresentative sample—i.e., only survivors. They exclude all who've died with an NEC-defining NDE, perhaps billions. So, their results can be skewed.

When Is an NEC a Natural Afterlife? All types of experiences can provide the last moment of an NEC. So precisely when would an NEC be *perceived* as an afterlife and thus be a natural afterlife? This is a tricky question, for the meaning of "afterlife" is a matter of semantics, perception is subjective, and what must be perceived is an issue. So, I'm going to cop out and just offer some thoughts.

Merriam-Webster defines "afterlife" as "an existence after death." As indicated before, all NECs include a sense of self to some degree—i.e., you will be the experiencer. Thus there's always "an existence" (i.e., immortality) from the dying person's perspective. So the most liberal answer to the question posed seems to be that every NEC is a natural afterlife. However, suppose one's last moment, likely an awake one, involves the thought, "I'm dying." It's hard to say this NEC is being perceived as an afterlife and thus to call it a natural afterlife.

The most conservative answer to the question may be that the NEC is a natural afterlife when it conforms to the dying person's view of what an afterlife might be like (e.g., they believe they're in Heaven). A less conservative answer is that though the dying person may not perceive the NEC as they envisioned an afterlife, the intensity of the sensuousness and emotionality of their final experience is such that they are completely captivated by it. This type of NEC experience is like that reported by Eben Alexander (2012a, 2012b). Could the experience be watching a beautiful sunset on the beach, perhaps with a loved one, or playing a great round of golf? Why not? Also, does one have to believe they've died? I say no. To rephrase this question, must one not only be perceiving an afterlife but be aware (i.e., self-aware) that they're perceiving an afterlife—i.e., an *after-death* existence? Again, I say no. Even in the commonly envisioned Heaven, I know of no requirement that one is aware of or remembers a past life or that they've died (except those imposed by some philosophers, as discussed in Chapter 5).

Though some may quibble with calling the natural afterlife an after*life* because it has no events, remember that the dying person doesn't know this, so to them, it is an afterlife—which, in the end, is what really matters.

Regarding the conservative answer as to when an NEC is a natural afterlife, what one perceives as an afterlife may be significantly influenced by religion. Masumian (2009) summarizes the afterlife teachings of predominant world religions and states that close examination of these teachings "reveals striking parallels between religious and near-death experience (NDE) accounts of [the] afterlife" (159). I discuss such parallels in Chapter 11.

A Logically Consistent, Optimal Heaven

When the NEC is a natural afterlife, it concludes an etna. If the etna is perceived as a heaven, then unlike most conventionally envisioned heavens (e.g., Heaven), it will be logically consistent. Not only that, it can be optimal in terms of eternal happiness.

Since $\Delta t = 0$ for the natural afterlife, at the end of the etna, one is just "living" in the moment. Thus, no decisions can be made (since there's no time for such); hence, free will is not an issue (i.e., irrelevant). Also, in a heavenly natural afterlife, one can never *become* bored because, again, $\Delta t = 0$. Boredom takes time.

In contrast, in the conventional, time-perceiving ($\Delta t > 0$) Heaven, which by definition implies a *perfect* heaven ("a place or condition of utmost happiness" according to *Merriam-Webster*), free will is problematic. It's actually impossible because bad decisions would introduce imperfection, dissatisfaction, unhappiness on the part of some, and perhaps even evil. Though without free will in such an infinite ($\Delta t = \infty$) heaven, boredom is almost inevitable because there will be no decisions to make and no challenges (as everything is already perfect). In such a place, what will one do for billions of years?

Thus, any eternal afterlife involving a time-perceiving consciousness must be either imperfect or logically inconsistent. The conventionally envisioned Heaven is the latter. In contrast, within a heavenly etna, one can logically experience—i.e., "live" in—a forever, perfect moment at its natural afterlife conclusion.

Indeed, *an etna provides not only a logical heaven but also an optimal heaven of utmost happiness*. But if only a "perfect *moment*," how can this be so? Because, as argued below, the etna is an eta—i.e., eventually timeless afterlife. It allows activities to occur in one's final experience that climax into a moment of utmost happiness, and once this happens, the moment becomes timelessly eternal with death.

An optimal heaven is possible given the highly pleasurable features of many reported NDEs and the natural afterlife's timeless, eternal, spiritual, and personalized aspects. However, claiming an optimal heavenly etna may seem incredible since, in concluding with a natural afterlife, nothing else happens!

As humans, we are so addicted to happenings—i.e., events and thus human time—that it's hard to appreciate the happiness possible in an eventless afterlife. We think we need events (i.e., perceived change) to make us eternally happy—hence the irrational longing for the supernaturally *perfect, everlasting, and yet ever-changing* afterlife. But do we really need events?

Do life's events give us pleasure, or is it the feelings and emotions that they arouse? The natural afterlife can be a moment where—based on past, say, NDE activities and events—you are left sensuously and emotionally in an extraordinarily intense and pleasurable final moment. Perhaps you know you're in Heaven, immersed in love (in the absolute presence of God as a theist may believe). Once this happens, precisely what more needs to happen? Indeed, once you achieve a moment of utmost happiness, more activities can never increase it but only potentially decrease it. This risk of less happiness may be especially high if free will is left to decide one's future activities. Asserted another way:

> *Once utmost happiness has been achieved by the feelings and emotions aroused by the events occurring in a time-perceiving afterlife, more time (i.e., events) can never result in more happiness, but only risk less.*

Below I repeat the assertion about the logical inconsistency of a time-perceiving, perfect, eternal afterlife.

> *Any eternal afterlife where a time-perceiving consciousness survives death must be either imperfect or logically inconsistent.*

The above two assertions are the basis for the *eta principle*:

> *Any afterlife that is perfect—i.e., provides utmost eternal happiness—must be an <u>e</u>ventually <u>t</u>imeless <u>a</u>fterlife (eta).*

With utmost happiness, one has to assume that the experiencer has no thought it will end. In the NEC, one does not know that nothing more will happen—i.e., there will be no next moment. Thus, in a heavenly etna of utmost happiness, humanly habituated by the experience of time always marching on, one is left in a state of exuberant, forever unspoiled anticipation of many more heavenly moments to come. That such anticipation contributes to a moment of utmost happiness is conveyed by the saying, "Anticipation is greater than realization,"

A Natural Afterlife Not Guaranteed

The NEC theory doesn't guarantee a natural afterlife. The percentage of people that die following an NDE, the experience most likely to result in a natural afterlife, is unknown. The percentage of near-death survivors reporting an NDE varies widely among studies (Zingrone & Alvarado 2009, 35). A 1981-82 study found that 47% of near-death survivors of attempted suicide reported an NDE, a high result relative to other studies. Three studies in 1995, 2001, and 2003 that involved a large number of cardiac arrest survivors showed that 18% to 23% of them reported NDEs. Studies of survivors *thought* "near-death" likely underestimated the frequency of NDEs among the dying because some may not have wished to divulge their NDEs. More significantly, some may not have been *near-death* enough to have one. Reports of NDEs will likely grow as advances in medicine—e.g., cardiopulmonary resuscitation (CPR)—continue (Brennan 2014, 329; Holden, Greyson, & James 2009a, jacket summary).

But will *I* die having an NDE? Perhaps comforting for some to know is that based on one study, NDEs may be bestowed without bias (Holden, Long, & MacLurg 2009). After reviewing much research on the characteristics of NDEr—e.g., age, sex, race and ethnicity, education, religious affiliation and religiosity, sexual orientation, or psychological factors—the study concluded that NDEs appear to be "equal opportunity transpersonal experiences" and so "everyone is a potential NDEr."

Remember that ELDVs may also result in a natural afterlife.

Applicable to Other Creatures

As previously stated in Chapter 2, the NEC theory applies to any "creature with human-like time and conscious perception." Extensive discussion of and firm conclusions about such applicability are unwarranted here. However, a brief overview of some current scientific thinking related to consciousness in nonhuman animals should provide some insight. So here are some findings:

Based on McNally et al. (2013), the question is no longer whether many vertebrates perceive time as a sequence of events but at what rate they process and resolve them. This resolution must occur in discrete units given binary neural firing, as in the visual system.

The Cambridge Declaration on Consciousness (Low et al. 2012) states: "Convergent evidence indicates that non-human animals have ... conscious states along with the capacity to exhibit intentional behaviors." and "the weight of evidence indicates that humans are not unique in possessing the neurological substrates that generate consciousness."

Dewey (2017) states: "Animal awareness, whatever it is like, must be more immediate and reactive [vs. human]. ... Animals must live more 'in the moment'" and "When it comes to emotions, there is more reason to think our states of mind resemble those of animals."

Pachniewska (2015) lists the many animals that have passed the *mirror test*. This test was developed in 1970 by psychologist Gordon Gallup Jr. to determine self-recognition.

Research has revealed that REM sleep, conducive to dreaming, occurs in higher-level mammals, including rats (Bekoff 2012; Louie & Wilson 2001).

Also, as mentioned in Chapter 6, research has revealed that rats have shown a surge in brain activity just before death, which could indicate NDEs (Borjigin et al. 2013).

And finally, a comprehensive report conducted by INRA, Europe's top agricultural research institute, notes that "in poultry, hens can judge their own state of knowledge suggesting they are conscious of what they know or do not know. Pigs can remember what events they experienced, where, and when." It concludes that "there is evidence that animals have knowledge of their own state (bodily self). They have the capacity to know and deal with their own knowledge, and also to evaluate the psychological state of their conspecifics, potentially leading to some form of empathy." (Le Neindre et al. 2017, 5)

Given all of the above, one might conclude that there is indeed a dog heaven after all, and perhaps one for other creatures as well.

Strengthened Validity Via Explanatory Power

In Chapter 9, I make the case that the NEC theory is a scientific theory and thus has the validity afforded to such a theory. A theory's validity is further strengthened by showing its explanatory power. This is accomplished by pointing out a theory's ability to effectively explain its relevant subject matter and account for, be consistent with, and perhaps even aid in understanding other closely related facts, observations, or phenomena. I do this below for the NEC theory.

First, based on the previous section, the theory provides the best hope for, is consistent with, and aids in understanding a closely related and often wished-for phenomenon. That would be a heaven for your dog, cat, or perhaps other beloved pet.

Second, the NEC theory offers greater explanatory power related to the existence of an afterlife than that provided by other theories. The etna, which the NEC makes possible, is natural—i.e., supported by science—and is logically consistent. Because it's logical and eventually timeless, it can provide the optimal heaven, not just one that's optimal for a while but then diminishes because of someone's not-so-good free will decision. Given its scientific basis, logicalness, and religious neutrality, the NEC theory should make belief in an afterlife possible even for the most ardent non-believer.

Third, for those who believe in and desire a hereafter that's justly based on one's behavior in life or beliefs, the NEC theory can provide one. For the religious, the NEC provides a stage for a paranormal agency (e.g., a God) to determine one's hereafter with justice and perhaps mercy. After all, the content of one's NEC, especially given ELDVs and NDEs, seems beyond one's control. Chapter 11 discusses the compatibility of the NEC with religious beliefs about the afterlife. However, is there a paranormal agent? For the non-religious, the NEC provides a stage for nature to take its course. However, does nature as we know it—science and psychology—only provide the stage? Will nature's causality and nondeterminism provide a just producer and director?

Fourth, for those who don't believe in (or even desire) a hereafter that's based on one's beliefs or behaviors, the NEC theory can *still* provide one. For example, dying peacefully and contently in one's last awake moments can result in resting peacefully and contently forever. Also, one can die forever paused in the pleasantry (or unpleasantry) of one's imagination, ELDV, or NDE. However, might the influence of a paranormal agent or nature affect these unconditional or perhaps unjust hereafters?

Fifth, the NEC theory is explanatory of a purpose for the existence of visions, dreams, and NDEs and is supported by their amazing characteristics. The lifetime-in-eternal model (to be presented in Chapter 7) was developed to emphasize their role in our lives. In these spiritually altered states of consciousness, we experience objects, events, thoughts, and emotions just as we do in our sensory reality (see Figure 5.3). While in them, we never lose our sense of self. We are ourselves, no one else. We are always the main character. We often can't distinguish our spiritual states from our sensory reality state. (The one exception is the rare lucid dream, wherein the dreamer knows they are dreaming.)

The ability of our minds to create these non-sensory realities (see Chapter 5) is an incredible, little-understood, and under-appreciated phenomenon. Though we are the main character in these realities, we are certainly not in control. Our mind seems to have "a mind of its own." Moreover, in creating them, our self seems to be our super self. Our mind can instantaneously paint before-unvisited, beautiful landscapes, design and decorate rooms, form new faces, compose plots and events, and create dialogue. Such rapid creativity is well beyond our talents and abilities while awake. These realities are indeed another dimension of being.

Why does such an incredible dimension exist? The NEC theory posits at least one answer, a momentous purpose—a natural afterlife, perhaps evolved in conjunction with our evolved intellect, senses, and emotions. Science, on the other hand, has yet to provide a better answer. While other purposes for dreaming have been posited, no scientific theory exists (Breus 2015; Lewis 2014). Moreover, science has advanced no purpose for NDEs and none for dreams or NDEs that are commensurate to their amazing features or as meaningful as the natural afterlife.

Sixth, the NEC theory—while independent of the explanations for NDEs, be they scientific or paranormal—is consistent with the scientific explanations for their existence and frequency. Though these explanations were given to refute claims that NDEs provide an afterlife, as discussed in Chapter 2, ironically, they facilitate the existence of a natural afterlife based on NDEs. Also, according to some scientists, our brains seem to have a natural propensity for producing NDEs. The following few paragraphs elaborate on these points.

Again, many articles in popular scientific publications have provided explanations for NDEs, essentially involving brain physiology. For example, Choi (2011)—in "Peace of Mind: Near-Death Experiences Now Found to Have Scientific Explanations" and primarily based on Mobbs & Watt (2011)—describes the common features of NDEs and explains how each might be the result of "normal brain function gone awry." He suggests they can be caused by: certain diseases, artificially stimulating parts of the brain, high-level releases of a stress hormone in the brain during trauma, medicinal and recreational drugs that similarly affect the brain as does trauma, and the depletion of blood and oxygen flow that can happen with extreme fear and oxygen loss when dying. Choi's first sentence states his central thesis: "Near-death experiences are often thought of as mystical phenomena, but research is now revealing scientific explanations for virtually all of their common features." The implicit claim here is that NDEs *do not* provide evidence of an afterlife. This claim is made explicit in the title of an article by Kyle Hill (2012), "The Death of 'Near Death': Even If Heaven Is Real, You Aren't Seeing It."

These authors aimed to explain NDEs as a natural phenomenon, not proof or evidence for any afterlife. However, the assumptions made by Choi, Hill, Shermer (2013), and many others (as cited in Chapter 2) are that an afterlife must begin after death and be time-perceiving. Remove these assumptions, and the research that supports the *materialistic* explanations for NDEs is ironically consistent with and supports the likelihood of having a *psychological*, timeless, natural afterlife that begins before death.

As mentioned in Chapter 1, observations and research studies support the brain's propensity to create NDEs and ELDVs. Some of these studies involved monitoring electroencephalographic (EEG) activity within the brains of dying patients. One study found that an end-of-life electrical surge (ELES) of unknown cause, perhaps indicative of an NDE, was commonly detected in the brains of a sample of critically ill patients who died (Chawla et al. 2017). In this study, the Patient State Index™ (PSI), which measures the level of sedation in anesthetized patients, was used to measure consciousness.

In another study, palliative care physician Michael Barbato (Barbato et al. 2017) obtained similar results when monitoring ELESs. The study was motivated by observations that:

> The time from unresponsiveness until death varies, and the decline is occasionally interrupted by episodes of unexpected lucidity even in the final moments of life.[8] Visible evidence includes a fleeting smile, eye opening, gestures, shedding of tears (lacrima mortis), and deathbed visions. *(e1)*

Thirty dying patients were connected to an EEG monitor that processed input from the frontal cortices to compute a Bispectral Index Score (BIS). This score, which is slightly different from the PSI, was used to measure the level of awareness. It, like PSI, is commonly used to measure the level of sedation in anesthetized patients. It ranges from 0 to 100, where 100 represents full awareness, 50 is heavy sedation, and 0 is *brain death*, which is the "complete loss of brain function" (Martin 2018). Similar to the Chawla et al. (2017) study, the striking finding was an inexplicable increase in BIS scores immediately before death. More specifically, an average spike of 31 (range 10 to 65) above baseline BIS was seen in 20 of the 30 patients.

Figure 6.1 shows the spike seen for one of the patients. Does it represent the conscious moments within an ELDV or NDE, perhaps this person's etna? Despite spikes reaching levels typically indicating almost full arousal, no subject in the study appeared awake or aware—aware, that is, from a material perspective.

Finally, the extreme intensity and reality of the experience provided by most NDEs, as revealed by NDE researchers (Brumfield 2013; Noyes, Fenwick, & Holden 2009; Thonnard et al. 2013),

---

[8] Wholihan, D. Seeing the light. End-of-life experiences—visions, energy surges, and other death bed phenomena. Nurs Clin North Am 2016; 51:489-500.

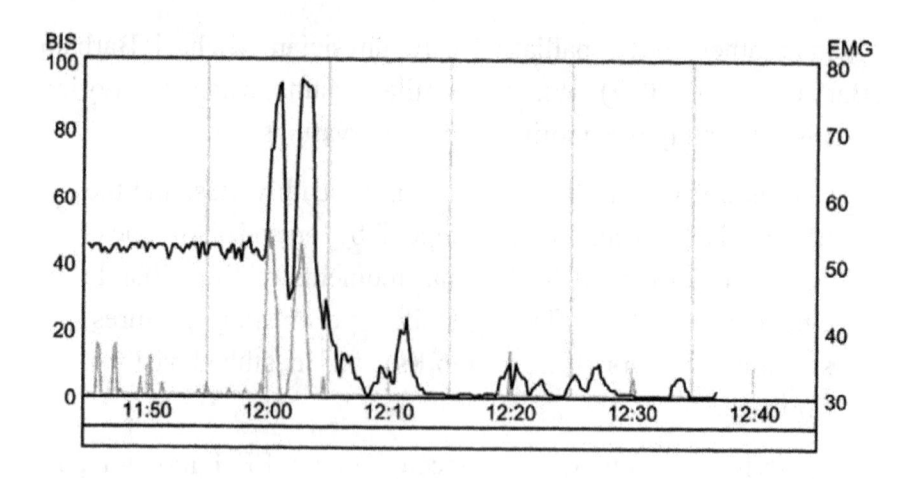

Figure 6.1. A representative tracing of a palliative care patient showing a spike in BIS (Bispectral Index Score) just before its rapid fall, signifying the moment of death. Also being traced (the grey line) is EMG (electromyographic activity). The baseline BIS for this dying patient is about 45, with a spike of about 50. (*e2*)

deserves special mention here because it begs the question: "Why such an intense, all too real, dreamlike experience just before death?" Again, science has no answer. But the NEC theory provides one. How better to imprint the awareness of one's final moment into the mind so that it will be a truly forever "unforgettable" present? Of course, forgetting is not an issue with the NEC. Instead, it's the amount of sensation, feeling, and emotion that an NDE packs into that last moment. An NDE can undoubtedly pack in much more than what might normally be present in one's last awake moment when passing out on their deathbed.

The last three arguments for the NEC theory's explanatory power involved NDEs. The remainder of this section provides a more in-depth, scholarly discussion of the relevancy of the NEC theory to NDEs. It was motivated by a recently published book.

Gregory Shushan (2022), in his book *The Next World: Extraordinary Experiences of the Afterlife,* gives an unbiased overview of the explanatory theories for NDEs (34–42), all of which he deems inadequate. He states, "As with any area of scientific research, new explanatory models must be constructed to accommodate new information" (42). The NEC theory is one such model but is not mentioned in the book. While the theory doesn't explain how NDEs are produced, it validates the *survival hypothesis* related to NDEs, which essentially states that the NDE is an afterlife. The NEC theory explains how NDEs are effectively a "glimpse into another world" (certainly not our materialistic one) and a "true spiritual reality" (23) and become a timeless "afterlife state" with death (228). In other words, according to the theory, *the NDE survives as an NEC and, possibly, an etna!*

Regarding the validity of the survival hypothesis, Shushan (2022, 227–254) discusses the fact that NDE researchers have viewed NDEs as both a universal human experience and an entirely culturally constructed one. The former view emphasizes the common features that most NDEs share, and the latter view emphasizes the differences in NDEs based on the culture of the NDEr. Shushan states that arguments for and against the survival hypothesis have been based on both views. He then provides an extensive overview of this simmering debate and offers his opinions.

The NEC theory is very relevant to this debate. It essentially "throws a wet blanket on it" by explaining that the NDE "is what it is" and most likely for a reason. The theory doesn't address what is materially versus paranormally versus culturally created in the NDE or why. Whatever the mixture, it's irrelevant to the *survival* of the NDE as an NEC and possibly an etna. Whatever is embodied in the last NDE moment *survives* death imperceptibly paused in the NDEr's mind. However, while cultural differences in NDEs are not relevant to NDE survival, they may contribute much to the personalization of the NEC. Indeed, cultural customization is likely needed to provide the utmost happiness in any etna. After all, what makes one extremely happy in one culture is often not the same as in another.

The survival debate will continue for those who persist in viewing the NDE as an after-death, eternal, time-perceiving experience. It will never be settled unless evidence reveals clear-cut cases of surviving NDErs having been in a time-perceiving state of consciousness *after brain death*.[9]

---

[9] Those viewing NDEs as after-death experiences assume NDErs don't need a functioning brain and that NDEs are reported by those who've died and come back to life. But, if true, why are there NDErs who have not been anywhere near death and why don't more NDErs come back to life past the point of any doubt they had died?

Part II
Analysis, Formal Definitions, and Validity

The devil is in the details.
—Anonymous

In this part, I get into the technicalities of analysis, formal definition, deduction, and testing to make a more scholarly case for the NEC theory's validity.

But why all the complexity—the diagrams, mathematics-like notation, and their explanations (all involving ugh!, *variables*)—when, as I stated in Chapter 1, "if one can just put themselves into the mind of a dying person ... then the NEC as a psychological phenomenon should be obvious"? First, being a computer scientist, the diagrams and notations helped me to analyze, better understand, and precisely describe the NEC theory and its related concepts. It's how I think and perhaps an excellent example of the value of a multidisciplinary approach.

Second, and most importantly, I believe an earth-shattering revelation such as the NEC theory must be supported by thorough analysis, formality, and preciseness in definition, deduction, and testing prescriptions. This support is what a new or major enhancement to a computer system should receive before incurring the cost of its implementation. Why should a significant and radical new afterlife theory deserve anything less? So, I feel the technicality is worthwhile, but you may skip this part of the book if you wish. I believe you will still have a good understanding of the NEC.

Chapter 7

The Lifetime-in-Eternity Model
A Product of Analysis

The lifetime-in-eternity model facilitates a precise and formal definition of the NEC and natural afterlife and the deduction of the NEC theory, given in the next chapter. The model accounts for every conscious moment and all periods of psychological timelessness related to a human's life within the context of time eternal. The model is the product of an analysis of the different types of conscious and unconscious (i.e., timeless) states of mind through which we pass—before, during, and after life. It was developed with "tools"—i.e., diagrams and notations—often used in computer science and software engineering.

The model is a system model and, like most system models, is abstract. This means that not every detail of the system being modelled is represented. What is represented is what is relevant to some application or subject matter. Here the subject is the periods (i.e., states of mind) wherein one alternates throughout life between perceiving time and not perceiving time and the events that transition one into and out of these states.

The lifetime-in-eternity model is presented at two levels of abstraction, the event level and moment level, because each level is best modelled using a different tool. The model defines experiences, which take place in conscious states, wherein each experience contains activities, each activity contains events, and each event contains moments. The types of experiences are awake experiences, dreaming experiences, and NDEs. Awake experiences are further divided into real, imaginary, and hallucinatory. Here "real" means alert—i.e., experiencing sensory reality as described in Chapter 5. Imaginary generally means "deep in thought" and not tuned into one's environment, perhaps recalling an experience. Hallucinatory experiences are the visionary experiences denoted by the V in ELDV, which can occur at other times besides the end of life (EL).

At its most detailed level, the model provides a representation of the last moment of the last event of the last activity of our final conscious experience, followed by the final period of timelessness. This period of timelessness is like all others within a lifetime—except that, from the perspective of the dying person, it never ends.

The Event Level

Figure 7.1 is a state diagram that presents the model at the highest level of abstraction. The state diagram is an analysis and modeling tool often used in computer science and software engineering to clarify the precise processing states within a system and the events that cause transitions between them. The system could be a manual (e.g., an inventory system), an old computer system, or a new one to be developed. Here the "system" being analyzed and modelled is the human mind.

The model in Figure 7.1 represents a life sandwiched between the before-life and the after-life. The model shows the major states of mind, both awake and not awake, and the events that cause the

THE LIFETIME-IN-ETERNITY MODEL

transitions between them. The states are represented by ovals and the events by arrows, both descriptively labelled. State names begin with a capital letter, and event names with a lowercase letter. In the state **After-life with NEC**, brackets denote that the NEC *could* be perceived as a **Natural Afterlife**. A state can be internal to (i.e., a substate of) another state. A time-perceiving state has an event arrow that loops from and back into the state. Events of the type given occur one or more times within (i.e., internal to) the state. Time is perceived to flow within such states as a stream of these

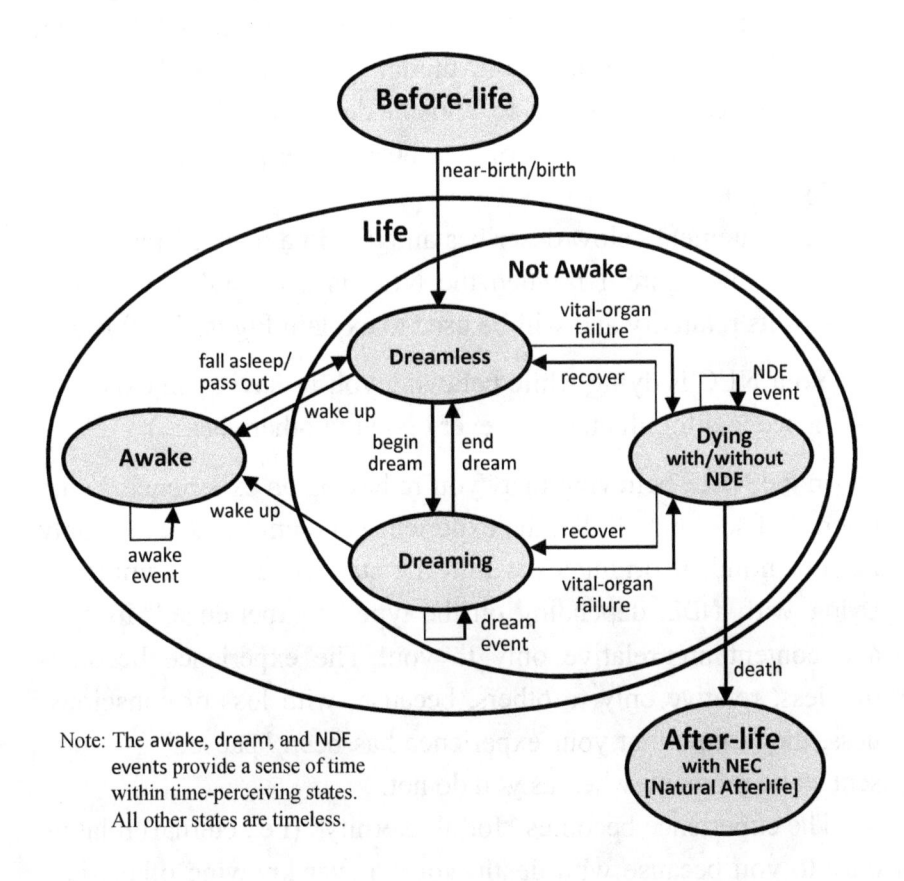

Note: The awake, dream, and NDE events provide a sense of time within time-perceiving states. All other states are timeless.

Figure 7.1. A state diagram providing the lifetime-in-eternity model at the highest level of abstraction. States of mind are denoted by ovals and state transitioning events by arrows.

perceived events. Timeless states have no such looping arrows, as no events are perceived within them. The looping arrow on the Dying state is applicable only when Dying with NDE. Event arrows that point from one state to another represent *imperceptible* events.

The word "Dying" and the term "vital-organ failure," the transitioning event into the Dying state, lack precise definitions. The vital-organ failure event is assumed to be a point at which failure within some organ (e.g., cardiac arrest) causes deterioration of brain cells and related brain functioning such that a person is now dying and near death. The event has likely already caused a person to pass out if still awake and is assumed to be such that the brain can no longer sustain a dream, though an NDE is still possible. This event can be equated to clinical death, which "is typically identified with the cessation of heartbeat and respiration" (Lexicon 2022).

The statement below describes an NEC in a nutshell (as literally shown in Figure 1.1 when the NEC is a natural afterlife). It stresses its relativity and will be used to explain Figure 7.1 further.

> Your NEC is dying while believing you're having an experience and for all eternity never knowing otherwise.

In the NEC, believing that "you're having an experience," with a sense of self and all that the experience encompasses, exists only in your mind. It originates within the state Awake, Dreaming, or Dying with NDE, depending on the type of experience.[10] Its type and content are relative only to you. The experience becomes timeless, relative only to others, because, with loss of consciousness, they know that your experience has been "paused" in a present static moment, whereas you do not.

The experience becomes "for all eternity" (i.e., eternal) relative only to you because with death, your "never knowing otherwise"

---

[10] The rare NDE that in not experienced near-death can be assumed as taking place in the Dreaming state of the lifetime-in-eternity model.

THE LIFETIME-IN-ETERNITY MODEL

extends beyond the originating state into the **After-life with NEC** state, transitioning via imperceptible events through one or more timeless states. If, for example, you never wake up after a dream, an **end dream** event will transition you into the **Dreamless** state, a vital-organ failure into the **Dying without NDE** state (assuming none), and **death** into the **After-life with NEC** state. What "you never know otherwise" (but the living know) is that your experience has ended—i.e., there will be no next conscious moment.

It is an opportune time to restate the following: Your NEC will be imperceptibly timeless and deceptively eternal to you, making it an illusion—but quite significantly, only to the living, not you.

Figure 7.2 reveals the states and events internal to the **Awake** state. The events into and out of the **Awake** state are the same as those in Figure 7.1. Three substates and six types of **begin–end**

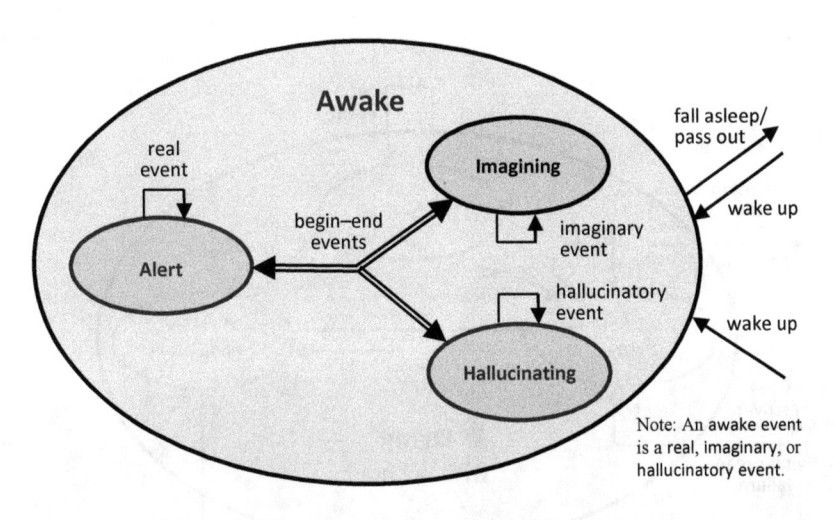

Figure 7.2. The states and transitions internal to the **Awake** state. Three substates are shown corresponding to three types of awake consciousness. Each state has two "**begin–end**" event pairs, each indicating transitions from (**begin**) and into (**end**) one of the other two states. For simplicity, all these events are shown as three two-line arrows with a common starting point.

events reflect that when we are awake, our minds seamlessly and imperceptibly transition among reality, imagination, and, hopefully rarely, hallucination. Thus, in the **Awake** state, we perceive time in terms of real events, imaginary events, and hallucinatory events, any of which can provide the final conscious moment for the NEC. Again, imagining can include daydreaming, recalling an experience, or just being deep in thought, oblivious to real events.

Figure 7.3 reveals the internals of the **Dying** state that are relevant to the NDE and the discussion of the NEC theory's testability, which is given in Chapter 9. The events transitioning one into and out of the **Dying** state in Figure 7.3 are the same as those in Figure 7.1. Three substates are identified. **Without NDE** is the state wherein a person is not having an NDE. **With NDE** is the state wherein a person is having an NDE. The **Severely Failing Brain** state reflects that dying is a gradual process that ends only at brain death when

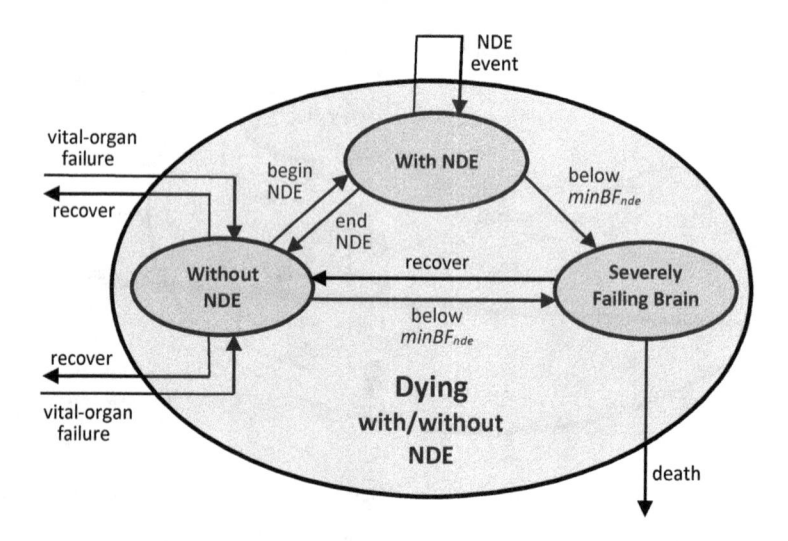

Figure 7.3. The states and transitions internal to the **Dying** state. The substates are shown that are relevant to the NDE and the testability of the NEC theory. $minBF_{nde}$ is the minimum brain functionality needed for an NDE.

no sign of brain activity is detected. This state is entered when the deterioration of brain function is such that the brain cannot support an NDE, regardless of whether the dying person is having one. The event named below *minBF$_{nde}$*, meaning below <u>min</u>imum <u>B</u>rain <u>F</u>unctionality (*minBF*) for an NDE, is defined as this point in time.

Note the assumption that the brain plays a role in producing the NDE. That is, the NDEr is not dead, as some believe. Death is not a prerequisite for an NDE as some NDErs are not even near death.

The Moment Level

The lifetime-in-eternity model presented so far describes a lifetime at the *event* level. Table 7.1 defines a formal notation, the *NEC notation*, that extends the model by taking this description down to the *moment* level—i.e., breaking down life's events into moments. It permits every conscious moment of a life and all periods of timelessness before, within, and after a life to be represented. However, to do so in complete detail would typically require billions of characters. This section explains Table 7.1.

The notation is defined using a technique typically used to define the syntax of formal languages (e.g., computer programming languages). Its primary purpose is to formally and precisely define the NEC and natural afterlife in the context of life and time eternal. Another is to stress that one's final conscious moment as a perceived present is just like all other conscious moments in life that immediately precede periods of timelessness.

As discussed in Chapter 4, perceived events are made up of static conscious moments. A sequence of such moments provides our stream of consciousness—one moment replacing another as our present moment, like one frame of a film replacing another as the projected one or one car of a train replacing another as the one immediately in front of you at a railroad crossing.

A NATURAL AFTERLIFE DISCOVERED

Table 7.1
The NEC Notation of the Lifetime-in-Eternity Model

Syntax. To represent all conscious moments and periods of timelessness before, within, and after a life, begin by traversing the railroad diagram labelled **Eternity**. When traversing a diagram, follow the arrows taking the proper paths as needed. When you come to a term in bold (e.g., **Life** and **E** vs. *Before-life* and m_r), go to its defining diagram, traverse it, and when you come to its end, return back to the diagram you left and continue on. When you come to the end of **Eternity** (denoted by **|**), you are done and have already traversed the second last diagram, which formally defines the **NEC**, and if it is a **Natural Afterlife**, the last diagram, which formally defines the **Etna**.

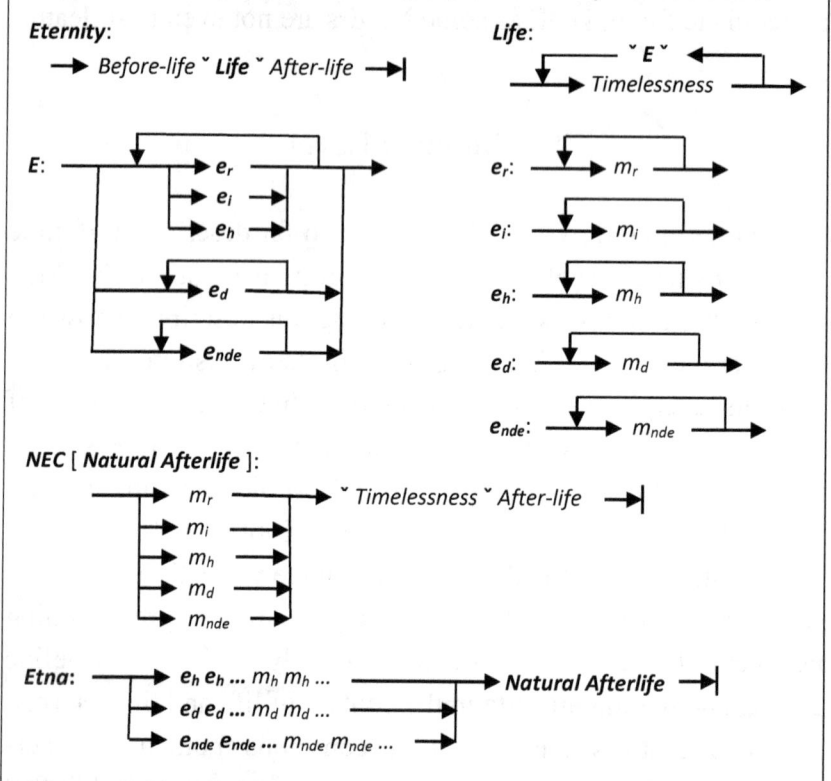

Eternity:

→ *Before-life* ˇ **Life** ˇ *After-life* →|

Life:

ˇ **E** ˇ
→ *Timelessness* →

E: e_r, e_i, e_h, e_d, e_{nde}

e_r: → m_r →
e_i: → m_i →
e_h: → m_h →
e_d: → m_d →
e_{nde}: → m_{nde} →

NEC [*Natural Afterlife*]:

→ m_r, m_i, m_h, m_d, m_{nde} → ˇ *Timelessness* ˇ *After-life* →|

Etna: → $e_h\, e_h\, ... \, m_h\, m_h\, ...$
$e_d\, e_d\, ... \, m_d\, m_d\, ...$
$e_{nde}\, e_{nde}\, ... \, m_{nde}\, m_{nde}\, ...$ → *Natural Afterlife* →|

Semantics. The paragraphs below define the meanings of all terms and symbols.

Eternity – time eternal as related to a lifetime. Specifically, the time before one's life (denoted by *Before-life*), followed by an imperceptible event (denoted by a ˇ), which here is birth or near-birth, followed by a lifetime (denoted by *Life*), followed by another imperceptible event ˇ, which here is death, followed by the time after one's life (denoted by *After-life*).

Life – a lifetime. Specifically, a period of real time in life wherein no events are perceived (denoted by *Timelessness*). This may (or may not) be followed one or more times by an imperceptible event (ˇ) that ends the timelessness (wake up, begin dream, or begin NDE), then an experience (denoted by **E**), and then another imperceptible

Table 7.1 (Continued)
The NEC Notation of the Lifetime-in-Eternity Model

event ($\check{\ }$) that again results in timelessness (e.g., fall asleep, pass out, end dream, or end NDE). The types of the two imperceptible events (e.g., begin dream and end dream) are consistent with the type of the experience (e.g., dream). *Timelessness* may occur over one or more contiguous timeless states of mind involving imperceptible transitioning events.

E – an experience of a type matching its perceived events. Specifically, a series of (one or more) awake events—which can be real, imaginary, or hallucinatory (i.e., visionary) events (each denoted by e_r, e_i, and e_h, respectively)—or a series of dream events (each denoted by e_d) or a series of NDE events (each denoted by e_{nde}).

e_r – an event consisting of a series of real conscious moments (each denoted by m_r). Ditto for e_i, e_h, e_d, and e_{nde} and a series of imaginary, hallucinatory, dream, and NDE conscious moments (each denoted by m_i, m_h, m_d, and m_{nde}), respectively.

NEC [*Natural Afterlife*] – the natural eternal consciousness (NEC), possibly a natural afterlife (denoted by the brackets). Specifically, the last moment of a *Life*—m_r, m_i, m_h, m_d, or m_{nde}—followed by an imperceptible event ($\check{\ }$) (e.g., pass out or end NDE) that results in *Timelessness* (possibly multiple periods) followed by another imperceptibel event ($\check{\ }$), here death, followed by the *After-life*.

Etna – the eventually timeless natural afterlife (etna). Specifically, a series of events where the last event can be interrupted after any moment by death. The events and the moments, including the last moment that begins the ***Natural Afterlife***, are all of the type hallucinatory, dream, or NDE.

Example. The notation below represents the end of a life (***Life***) and the after-life (***After-life***) that follows. A ... indicates zero or more like moments that are not shown. *Tln* is used as an abbreviation for *Timelessness*.

...$m_r m_r$...$m_r m_i m_i$...$m_i \check{\ } Tln \check{\ } m_d m_d$...$\underline{m_d \check{\ } Tln \check{\ }} m_r m_r$...$m_r \check{\ } Tln \check{\ } m_d m_d$...$m_d \check{\ } Tln \check{\ }$ After-life
|⟵ **NEC** ⟶|
[*Natural Afterlife*]
|⟵ [*Etna*] ⟶|

A person is awake, alert (m_rs) and imagining (m_is), falls asleep ($\check{\ }$), begins a dream ($\check{\ }$), dreams (m_ds), ends the dream ($\check{\ }$), wakes up ($\check{\ }$), is alert (m_rs), passes out ($\check{\ }$) with a heart attack, begins a dream ($\check{\ }$), dreams (m_ds), ends the dream ($\check{\ }$), and dies ($\check{\ }$). The ***NEC*** may be perceived as a ***Natural Afterlife***. Note that the m_d is perceived as the present in the ***NEC*** just as an m_d is perceived as such in the underlined *Tln*, except in the ***NEC*** it is perceived as the present forever because the person never wakes up.

If the ***NEC*** is perceived as a ***Natural Afterlife***, the preceding moments ($m_d m_d$...) and the ***NEC*** makeup the ***Etna***. The moments form the events (e_ds) that form the activities within the final dream experience (***E***). Note that the m_ds within the ***Etna*** could just as well have been m_hs or m_{nde}s within a final hallucination or NDE, respectively.

Coincidently, the NEC notation describes these moment "trains" and the periods of timelessness separating them using *railroad diagrams*. They define the syntax of the notation, and the "Syntax" part of Table 7.1 begins by giving directions for traversing them—i.e., following the tracks. The "Semantics" part gives the meaning of all terms and symbols used in them. The "Example" part shows the notation generated by traversing the diagrams to represent (or describe) the end of a particular lifetime.

The first eight railroad diagrams define a lifetime in the context of eternity using terms and symbols in a top-down manner (i.e., from general to specific). The terms are variables—e.g., **Life**, representing a life (any life), or m_r, representing a real (i.e., sensory) moment. A variable given in regular font is a terminal, meaning it's not defined further by another diagram. One that's bold is a nonterminal, meaning another railroad diagram defines it.

The first diagram, labelled **Eternity**, defines an eternity with respect to a **Life**. The ˇ symbol represents an imperceptible event. Here the first ˇ is birth or near-birth, and the second is death. These correspond to the same events shown in the state diagram in Figure 7.1. The | symbol at the end of this diagram indicates the end of all traversing. However, you must traverse the diagram to get to it, which means you must traverse the diagram for **Life**.

The diagram for **Life** defines a life in terms of the experiences (**E**s) and periods of *Timelessness*. A ˇ traversed after *Timelessness* and before **E** represents an imperceptible event that transitions one out of the timelessness, like wake up. A ˇ traversed after **E** and before *Timelessness* is an imperceptible event that transitions one back into timelessness, like fall asleep. After going round and round in this diagram as needed to generate and thus account for and describe all experiences within a lifetime, one must return to the **Eternity** diagram to encounter the *After-life*.

Diagram **E** defines an experience in terms of the perceived events (**e**s) that happen within it. The type of experience is defined by the type of events that comprise it—real (*r*), meaning awake and alert, imaginary (*i*), hallucinatory (*h*), dream (*d*), and NDE (*nde*).

A diagram for each event type defines it in terms of its moments (*ms*). The type of the moments is consistent with the type of the event. An experience (**E**) corresponds to the notion of the "moment train" as devised by Stroud (1955)—i.e., a sequence of discrete conscious moments within our stream of consciousness.[11]

The NEC notation below describes the beginning of a life, including two periods of dreamless sleep and two experiences.

Before-life˘Timelessness˘$m_r m_r$...m_r˘Timelessness˘$m_r m_r$...m_r˘

To generate it, one must traverse the diagram **Eternity** to get to **Life**. Go to diagram **Life** and traverse over ˘**E**˘ twice to get the two periods of dreamless sleep and two experiences. When at each **E**, go to diagram **E** and traverse over e_r one or more times. When at each e_r, go to diagram e_r and traverse over m_r one or more times. Traversing over a ˘ symbol or terminal (e.g., m_r) generates it.

Formal Definitions and an Example

If you traverse the diagrams as directed to represent some lifetime in eternity, you will eventually arrive at the | in the **Eternity** diagram. In the process, you have gone over (i.e., generated) likely billions of conscious moments (*ms*) and tens of thousands of periods of *Timelessness*. You have also already traversed the diagram for **NEC [Natural Afterlife]**. If the NEC was a natural afterlife (the possibility indicated by the brackets), you have already traversed the diagram for **Etna**. The former diagram formally defines the NEC and natural afterlife in the context of a life in eternity and is referred to hereafter as the *NEC_FD* (*NEC Formal Definition*). The latter diagram formally defines the etna.

The NEC_FD defines how all lives will end. That is, every person will always end up with—i.e., all tracks (or paths) lead to—one of these five possible representations for the end of their life:

---

[11] In the NEC notation, subscripts identify the type of event, not its position in a sequence as in Figure 4.1.

m_r ˘ *Timelessness* ˘ *After-life*
m_i ˘ *Timelessness* ˘ *After-life*
m_h ˘ *Timelessness* ˘ *After-life*
m_d ˘ *Timelessness* ˘ *After-life*
m_{nde} ˘ *Timelessness* ˘ *After-life*

m_r, m_i, m_h, m_d, and m_{nde} denote one's last conscious m̲oment—r̲eal, i̲maginary, h̲allucinatory (or visionary), d̲ream, and n̲d̲e̲ (NDE), respectively. m_r, m_i, and m_h are awake moments. Each type of moment encapsulates the sense of self and all sensory perceptions—whether those of a sensory or non-sensory reality (see Chapter 5)—present within the respective type of experience at its end. It also includes present thoughts, beliefs, and emotions, almost all of which linger from past moments (preceding *m*s) that make up the current and previous events of the experience. One such belief is, to some extent, that of a future—i.e., of future moments and events consistent with recent ones and the now-forever present one. Thus, in the dying person's mind, the *m* in the NEC$_{FD}$ represents the experience at a point in time.

The first ˘ in NEC$_{FD}$ denotes an imperceptible event that transitions one into *Timelessness*. The event is consistent with the type of the preceding moment. It can be **fall asleep, pass out, end dream, end NDE**, or an abnormal failure event occurring in a deteriorating brain. The latter event results in the brain no longer being able to produce another moment of the type being experienced—i.e., a **vital-organ failure** or below *minBF$_{nde}$* shown in Figures 7.1 and 7.3.

The *Timelessness* that then follows begins the imperceptible eternal timelessness that pauses one in their last moment. Specifically, it denotes the timelessness occurring over one or more timeless states leading up to and including the **Severely Failing Brain** substate (Figures 7.1 and 7.3). It then is followed by the timelessness of the **After-life** state—denoted in the NEC$_{FD}$ by *After-life*, where the preceding ˘ is the imperceptible event **death**.

The last three representations in the NEC$_{FD}$ listed above provide the possibility for a **Natural Afterlife** and etna. But again, it occurs only when the final experience—an hallucination, dream, or NDE—is perceived by the dying person as an afterlife. The **Etna** diagram in Table 7.1 formally defines the etna, and its traversal results in three possible representations:

$e_h\ e_h\ ...\ e_h\ m_h\ m_h$ ... **Natural Afterlife**
$e_d\ e_d\ ...\ e_d\ m_d\ m_d$ ... **Natural Afterlife**
$e_{nde}\ e_{nde}\ ...\ e_{nde}\ m_{nde}\ m_{nde}$ ... **Natural Afterlife**

The etna begins with the first event of the final experience—i.e., the first e_h, e_d, or e_{nde} listed above—and ends with the **Natural Afterlife**. The sequence of events that forms the last experience is shown, with the last one broken down into its discrete moments. These discrete moments are shown because the last event can be imperceptibly interrupted by the onset of death after any moment. The final moment of life—m_h, m_d, or m_{nde}—is not shown in the above representations because it's part of the **NEC** and **Natural Afterlife** and thus appears in the NEC$_{FD}$.

The etna is formally defined in the NEC notation in terms of its events and moments. It could have been defined only in terms of moments. (Indeed, traversing the ORN notation diagrams generates the moments for all events shown.) Note that Figure 5.1 describes the etna in terms of activities, events, and moments.

The types of **E** are not explicitly defined in Table 7.1—e.g., **E$_d$**. Each experience type could have been defined as a series of activities of the same type (e.g., **A$_d$**), each of which could have been defined as a series of events of the same type (e.g., **e$_d$**). This wasn't done as it would have added more complexity and wasn't needed to define the NEC and etna formally. However, the extra NEC notation given in Figure 7.4 defines each type of **E**, though not the corresponding types of activities. The figure and its caption also define the nonterminal **Timelessness** used in the next section.

E: ⟶ E_a
⟶ E_d
⟶ E_{nde}

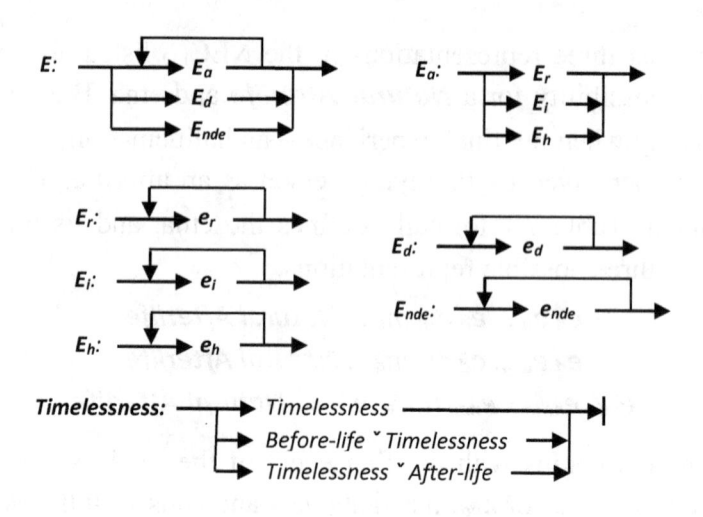

E_a: ⟶ E_r
⟶ E_i
⟶ E_h

E_r: ⟶ e_r

E_i: ⟶ e_i

E_h: ⟶ e_h

E_d: ⟶ e_d

E_{nde}: ⟶ e_{nde}

Timelessness: ⟶ Timelessness
⟶ Before-life ˇ Timelessness
⟶ Timelessness ˇ After-life

Figure 7.4. Extra NEC notation. The first seven diagrams are an equivalent definition to that in Table 7.1 for **E**. They explicitly identify the types of experiences: <u>a</u>wake, <u>r</u>eal, <u>i</u>maginary, <u>h</u>allucinatory, <u>d</u>ream, and NDE. The last diagram defines **Timelessness** (in bold), a period that may include the before-life or after-life wherein no events are perceived.

Besides allowing the NEC and etna to be formally defined, the NEC notation shows that, *cognitively*, the timelessness in the NEC with a conscious moment as the present throughout is the same situation that occurs numerous times in life. The NEC notation given in the Example part of Table 7.1 is duplicated below, where *Tln* abbreviates *Timelessness*. It describes a dying person's last few end-of-life experiences and their death and after-life.

$$...m_rm_r...m_rm_im_i...m_i \text{ˇ} Tln \text{ˇ} m_dm_d...\underline{m_d \text{ˇ} Tln} \text{ˇ} m_rm_r...m_r \text{ˇ} Tln \text{ˇ}$$
$$m_dm_d...m_d \text{ˇ} Tln \text{ˇ} After\text{-}life$$

For this person, perceiving the final m_d as the present throughout the NEC, denoted above as $m_d \text{ˇ} Tln \text{ˇ} After\text{-}life$, is the same as perceiving m_d as the present throughout the $m_d \text{ˇ} Tln$ that is underlined—which denotes a dream moment, an **end dream** event, and the timelessness that precedes waking up. The only difference is that the person wakes up from the underlined $m_d\check{\ }Tln$ to an awake moment—i.e., an m_r.

If this person's life concludes with an etna, it is one based on a dream; however, the ending sequence of m_ds (i.e., the moments for all final dream events) could instead have been m_hs or, more likely, m_{nde}s. Here, m_ds were chosen because this sequence occurs many times in life and forms the basis for probably the best thought experiment that allows the living to envision the NEC, natural afterlife, and etna—i.e., imagining never waking up from a dream.

A Summary of Concepts and Relationships

Figure 7.5 is a class diagram that describes the relationships among the concepts associated with the NEC theory. It's another product in my comprehensive NEC analysis, or perhaps over-analysis! Regardless, it serves as a summary and review and may be helpful for some.

The class diagram is often used as an analysis and modeling tool in computer science and software engineering in developing computerized systems. It identifies the types of objects (i.e., entities or things) that one must deal with in a particular system (e.g., an accounting system) and clarifies the terms used to describe them. The diagram also clarifies the relationships among them. A computer system must often store and maintain information on these objects in a database.

When used to analyze the NEC theory, the system is again the human mind, which has been "computerized" by the brain. The objects to be dealt with are all conceptual objects. In providing a different system perspective from the state diagrams and NEC notation, the class diagram in Figure 7.5 is part of the lifetime-in-eternity model.

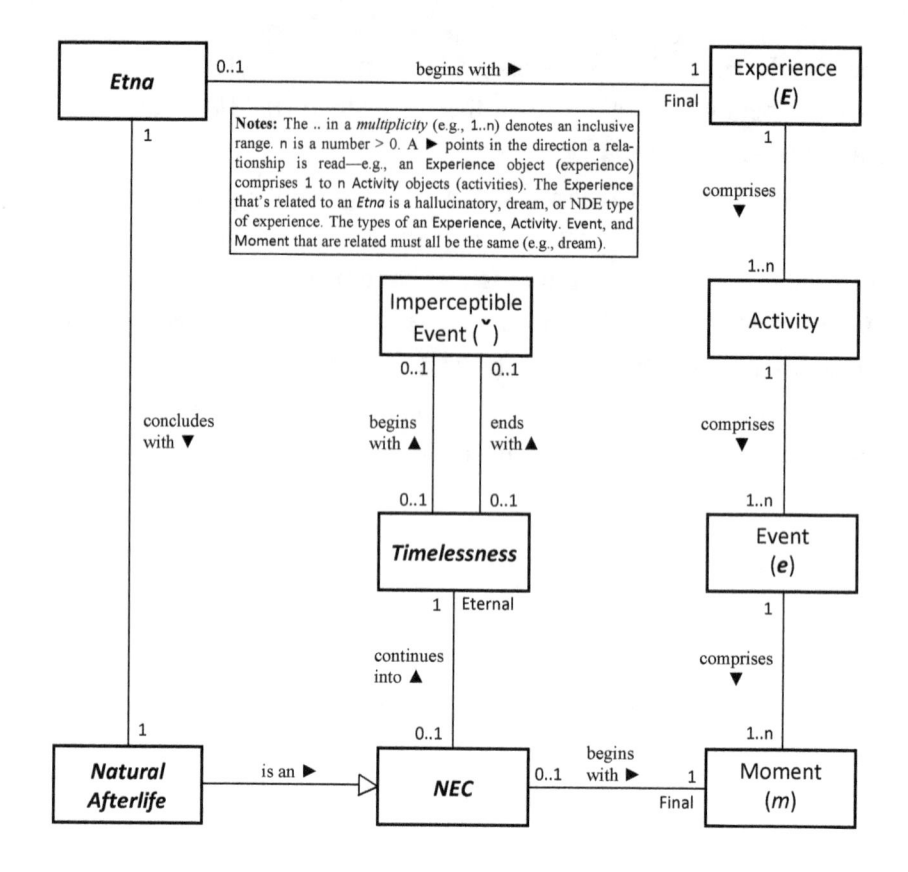

Figure 7.5. A class diagram that shows the relationships among terms associated with the NEC theory. A rectangle represents a class of objects (i.e., things) of the same type. The description in the rectangle identifies the class by describing the class object type. A line between two classes represents a relationship between the objects of each class. The labels and notations given on the line describe the type of relationship. Here, all classes and relationships are described in the context of one individual.

The diagram applies to one individual. In this context, while there can be many experiences per individual, there can only be one NEC, natural afterlife, and etna.

The caption for the figure gives a general description of the meanings of the rectangles and connecting lines in the class diagram. Rather than repeat these here, the diagram will simply be "read" as intended to convey these meanings, starting at the rectangle in the upper-left corner.

To begin the reading, an object of the class (i.e., type) **Etna** (an etna) "begins with" one (1) object of the class (i.e., type) Experience (an experience). In this relationship, this particular experience plays the role of the Final experience of an individual. Thus "Final" is a *role name* in the class diagram.

Note that each class description either corresponds to an NEC notation term (e.g., **Etna**) or is a more descriptive term (e.g., Experience or Imperceptible Event) for an NEC notation term or symbol (e.g., **E** or ˇ) that is given in parenthesis below it. Terms in bold are defined by railroad diagrams in the NEC notation.

An experience (**E**) can be of the type awake, dream, or NDE, where an awake experience can include real, imaginary, or hallucinatory events. These experience types are not made explicit in the class diagram. (Note that in the NEC notation, as given in Table 7.1, the type of an experience is implicit by the type of events that occur within it. In Figure 7.4, however, experience types are made explicit.)

A relationship is meant to be read in the direction of the readability indicator—i.e., arrowhead (▶). One can also read it in the reverse direction, provided they make the proper grammatical change to the relationship description. For example, an experience, as the Final experience, "begins" zero to one (0..1) etna. The .. denotes an inclusive range, but when the low and high numbers differ by 1, the .. is often read as "or," as in "zero or one." The 0 denotes that an experience may not "begin" an etna.

Now to read the other **Etna** relationship, an etna "concludes with" one (1) **Natural Afterlife**. Reading this relationship in the reverse direction: a natural afterlife "concludes" one (1) etna.

A natural afterlife "is an" **NEC**. The open arrowhead at the **NEC** end denotes the special "is a" type of relationship. Thus here, the "is an" description is redundant. The relationship is special because, unlike other relationships, the natural afterlife and NEC are not two different objects that are related but the same object. The direction of the arrowhead indicates that while a natural afterlife is an NEC, an NEC is not necessarily a natural afterlife.

An NEC "begins with" one (1) Moment (m), an individual's Final. Reading the relationship in reverse, not every moment "begins" an NEC, thus the 0..1.

An NEC "continues into" one period of **Timelessness**, the nonterminal defined in Figure 7.4. This period is identified as Eternal because, with death, it continues into the *After-life*. Each period of **Timelessness** "begins with" zero or one (0..1) imperceptible event (ˇ) (e.g., **fall asleep**) and "ends with" zero or one (0..1) imperceptible event (e.g., **wake up**). The 0.. is needed for both relationships only because the **Timelessness** that starts with the *Before-life* isn't assumed to begin with an imperceptible event and the one that ends with the *After-life* isn't assumed to end with one.

Now to go back to **Experience**, an experience "comprises" one to many (1..n) activities. n represents an unlimited number and is usually read as "many" or "more." Activities are not part of the NEC notation. An activity comprises one or more events; thus, by transitivity, an experience comprises one or more events (as denoted in the NEC notation). Here, an *Event* (**e**) is a *perceived* event. A perceived event comprises one or more conscious moments (*ms*).

Now to finish the reading with some backtracking and conclude this chapter: in reverse, starting at **Moment**, one moment, but only the **Final** one of a lifetime, "begins" (the reverse of "begins with") an NEC, which "may be" a natural afterlife. If so, this afterlife "concludes" (the reverse of "concludes with") an etna. According to the NEC theory, this is reality. Establishing it as such is the subject of the following two chapters. Accepting and dealing with it is a philosophical and religious subject and is discussed in Part III of this book.

Chapter 8

Validity Via "Proof" by Deduction

In explaining how the NEC is possible in previous chapters, I have essentially already implicitly and informally deduced (i.e., "proven") its existence. However, in this chapter, I make it more explicit, formal, and rigorous.

Absolute Vs. Empirical Truths, Hypothesis Vs. Theory

But before proceeding with this "proof," I must first explain why I must put *proof*, *prove*, and *proven* in quotation marks. A proof is related to and required for a logical, mathematical, or computational theorem. Such theorems are proven based on *absolute truths*. Here, I am giving a "proof" based on *empirical truths*, which are truths that have been verified and generally accepted as true based on observation, experiment, or experience. However, the possibility remains that they could be shown to be false (i.e., falsified) or at least so in some cases in the future.

So I must point out some caveats related to my "proof" of the NEC theory. First, I establish that all propositions I use are indeed cognitive principles—meaning they're empirical truths, not absolute truths. Therefore, any conclusions deduced based on them can only be empirical truths.

Second, any conjunction of empirical truths can imply a scientifically sound empirical truth only so long as, when combined, they do not interact in some unexpected way. Experience has shown that vinegar is a good cleaner and bleach is a good disinfectant, which implies that combining them will result in a good cleaner and disinfectant. Right? Wrong! What we will get is a potentially lethal chlorine gas! I believe, however, it is safe to assume here that the three empirical truths used to "prove" the NEC theory do not interact in some unknown way (e.g., at a compositional level like vinegar and bleach) to negate their combined effect. The next section states these truths as cognitive principles.

Third, I assume a human "time and conscious perception," so the "proof" is valid only for humans. I discussed the theory's applicability to other creatures in Chapter 6.

Another issue I will address before proceeding is what is a hypothesis and what is a theory. Although these words have stricter meanings in a scientific context than in common usage, assumed scientific meanings are still sometimes at odds. For example, on the *Live Science* website, Bradford (2017) states:

> Every scientific theory starts as a hypothesis. A scientific hypothesis is a suggested solution for an unexplained occurrence that doesn't fit into a currently accepted scientific theory. ... If enough evidence accumulates to support a hypothesis, it moves to the next step—known as a theory—in the scientific method and becomes accepted as a valid explanation of a phenomenon.

On the other hand, Biologist T. Ryan Gregory (2008), in an article explaining the status of evolutionary theory, states:

> ... a theory in science, again following the definition given by the NAS [(1998)], is "a well-substantiated explanation of some aspect of the natural world that can incorporate facts, laws, inferences, and tested hypotheses." (47).

And he goes on to state that "hypotheses never become theories" (48). Either Bradford or Gregory seems to have "the cart before the horse," but which one?

In the introduction to Chapter 4, I gave a hypothesis, Hypothesis 2, and stated, "this book thoroughly analyzes Hypothesis 2 and promotes it to a scientific theory," that being the NEC theory. This promotion aligns with Bradford (2017) that a theory starts with a hypothesis. I assume this in the remainder of this chapter and the next. In Ehlmann (2020), I did it directly; however, in this chapter, I do it as a two-step process. First, I "prove" a more general theory, which does not address death. Then, based on this general theory, I "prove" the NEC theory as a hypothesis. This approach is consistent with Gregory (2008) that a hypothesis stems from a theory, not vice versa.

More specifically, in Ehlmann (2020), I establish the NEC theory as a scientific theory to explain—admittedly, with little detail—how an eternal consciousness and afterlife can be natural. It explains that this consciousness is "relative to the creature's perception, its final conscious moment ... and may be perceived as a natural afterlife." The more detailed explanation, however, based on cognitive science principles, is given in its deduction, or "proof." The PCT theory (i.e., the theory of a paused consciousness in timelessness) summarizes most of the cognitive science explanation, except that which addresses death. It is more general in that it addresses many situations in life. It is "proven" in the next section. Then, in the subsequent section, the NEC theory is "proven" as a hypothesis based on the PCT theory, claiming an NEC in the case of death. Here "proven" means supported by logical deduction based on empirical truths.

The PCT Theory: Statement and "Proof"

The PCT theory and a clarifying statement, as given before in Chapter 2, are repeated below.

The consciousness of a creature with human-like time and conscious perception is, relative to the creature's perspective, imperceptibly paused in its last conscious moment during periods of timelessness and resumed with its next conscious moment.

The last conscious moment is not remembered upon the resumption of consciousness. It need not be because it's still the present; however, soon afterward, it may be forgotten due to some combination of its being mundane and the creature's attention being immediately focused on subsequent moments and events.

Proof: The PCT theory can be inferred from three natural phenomena, which can also be viewed as cognitive principles. First is the perception of time as dependent on (i.e., relative to) a perceived, ordered sequence of events—real or otherwise. Call this *Event Relative Time*. Second is a consciousness—i.e., perception and awareness—that occurs *only* as a sequence of *static*, discrete conscious moments, *one present moment at a time*. The content of this present moment is such that past moments play a major role in shaping it and a consistent next moment, a future one, is always anticipated. Call this *Present Moment Consciousness*. Third is the inability to perceive the transition from a time-perceiving state into a timeless state. Call this *Imperceptible Loss of Time*. When each of these principles is treated as a proposition, the PCT theory can be logically stated as follows:

(*Event Relative Time* ∧ *Present Moment Consciousness*
  ∧ *Imperceptible Loss of Time*) → PCT Theory

VALIDITY VIA "PROOF" BY DEDUCTION

To "prove" this statement true, one must show that all three propositions in the conjunction (∧) and the implication (→) are true—i.e., empirically true.

The propositions *Event Relative Time* and *Present Moment Consciousness* as cognitive principles are well established by science and philosophy, as discussed in Chapter 4. Thus they are true (empirically, that is).

Now the *Imperceptible Loss of Time*, which is stated below as a cognitive principle and lemma, must be shown to be true. A lemma is a subsidiary proposition used to prove another proposition—here, the PCT theory.

The transition from a time-perceiving state into a timeless state of mind is imperceptible.

This principle is true for two reasons. First, clearly, no perceived event in the timeless state signals the transition (since the state is timeless and thus has no perceived events). And second, as I now argue by case, all types of events transitioning one into timeless states, identified in Figures 7.1 to 7.3, are imperceptible based on human experience or what is impossible given present scientific knowledge.

Human experience confirms that one never perceives
1. falling asleep—i.e., the **fall asleep** event;
2. passing out from fainting, drugs, trauma, or medical condition—i.e., the **pass out** event;
3. ending a dream—i.e., the **end dream** event; and
4. ending an NDE—i.e., the **end NDE** event.

Regarding events 1 and 2, though one may be groggy or with head trauma, "see stars," one only realizes these events occurred upon waking up. It's always "I must have fallen asleep." or "I must have passed out." but never "I've fallen asleep." or "I've passed out," respectively. Regarding 3, to belabor a point, you never know a dream has ended until you wake up. Regarding 4, though those who recover from an NDE may recall its final moments (even being told something like "You must return now."), they do not report any perceived moment signaling its end (Holden, Greyson, & James 2009a; Long 2010; Moody 2001).

Two other events shown in Figures 7.1 and 7.3 that can transition one into timelessness (or merely result in its continuance) are **vital-organ failure** and below *minBF$_{nde}$*. These, however, are purely physiological events that are imperceptible almost by definition. The first is defined to mean deterioration in brain functionality to such a level that dream events are impossible (even more so, awake events), and the second to mean further deterioration such that NDE events are impossible. How then can events like these be perceived in an unconscious state when such brain deterioration levels are reached—i.e., when, by definition, there can be no awake moment (m_r, m_i, or m_h), no m_d after a **vital-organ failure**; and no m_{nde} after a **below** *minBF$_{nde}$*? No evidence exists that anyone who has recovered from the ensuing timeless has ever perceived these two events. (In fact, whether they are even identifiable as precisely defined is questionable but not critical to this proof.)

Given that all possible transitioning events into timeless states are imperceptible, *Imperceptible Loss of Time* is empirically true.

Having established that all propositions are true, one must now show that the implication (→) is true.

Given *Event Relative Time*, at many points in life, one perceives an awake, dream, or NDE event (possibly interrupted after some moment) and immediately transitions from a time-perceiving state into timelessness. (This timelessness is modelled in Figures 7.1 and 7.3 as a path through a sequence of one or more states having no perceived events and denoted in the NEC notation by *Timelessness*).

Given the *Imperceptible Loss of Time*, one does not perceive any transitioning event into these timeless states (the ˘ preceding *Timelessness* in the NEC notation). Thus, within periods of timelessness, one does not perceive any event following their last conscious moment.

Finally, given this and *Present Moment Consciousness*, one does not perceive any conscious moment within periods of timelessness that changes their *unawareness* of the last conscious moment (an m_r, m_i, m_h, m_d, or m_{nde} in the NEC notation) as their last and thus their self-awareness of it as their present. Hence, *relative to one's perspective*, this last moment, embodying an experience, remains their present moment until another conscious moment changes their awareness. Moreover, this present moment is imperceptibly timeless to them because, as with all conscious moments, it's imperceptibly static.

Therefore, assuming no startling interactions among the three empirically true propositions (i.e., the causal phenomena), the implication ($\rightarrow$) is true. That is, one's consciousness is, from their perspective, imperceptibly paused during periods of timelessness in their last conscious moment and resumed with their next conscious moment. Thus, by thorough analysis and reasoning, the PCT theory is "proven"—i.e., deduced from empirical truths. ∎

The NEC Theory: Statement and "Proof"

As stated in Chapter 2, the NEC theory is given below, along with a clarifying statement.

> *The natural eternal consciousness (NEC) of a creature with human-like time and conscious perception is, relative to the creature's perception, its final conscious moment. The NEC may be perceived as a natural afterlife.*

> The final conscious moment is within a perceived event of a type known to be experienced by humans—real, imaginary, hallucinatory, dream, or NDE.

Proof: Though I still call it a theory, the NEC theory can be considered a hypothesis based on a more general theory. It meets the American Psychological Association's definition of a hypothesis as "an empirically testable proposition about some fact, behavior, relationship, or the like, usually based on theory, that states an expected outcome resulting from specific conditions ... " (APA 2020). The "theory" is the PCT theory. The "specific conditions" are a creature has human-like time and conscious perception, enters a period of timelessness, and then dies. The "expected outcome" and "fact" is that its final conscious moment becomes its NEC and possibly its natural afterlife.

As a hypothesis, the NEC theory is logically stated as follows:

$$(PCT\ Theory \land Imperceptible\ Death)$$
$$\rightarrow$$
$$(NEC \land [\ Natural\ Afterlife\ ])$$

The [ ]s denote the possibility of a Natural Afterlife—which, as previously discussed, is subjective. It is true by definition if the NEC is true and the NEC is perceived as an afterlife by the dying person (see Chapter 6)

The *PCT theory*, given as a proposition above, is true (based on its "proof") and clearly applicable to the NEC theory. For in dying, one perceives a last awake, dream, or NDE event (possibly interrupted after some conscious moment) and transitions into a period of timelessness lasting until death (modelled in Figures 7.1 and 7.3 as a path through a sequence of one or more timeless states up to and including the **Severely Failing Brain** state and denoted in the NEC$_{FD}$ by *Timelessness*). At this point, one is paused in their last present conscience moment based on the PCT theory.

Then, one encounters a new and final transitioning event (the event **death** shown in Figures 7.1 and 7.3 and denoted by the ˇ before *After-life* in the NEC$_{FD}$). The "no evidence exists" claim, used to argue that the **end dream** and **end NDE** events were imperceptible, clearly cannot be used in the case of **death**. The inability to perceive the moment of death, the proposition of an *Imperceptible Death*, can be seen as an extension of the *Imperceptible Loss of Time* proposition. This extension seems especially true given that brain functionality has deteriorated beyond that at which dream or NDE moments are possible. Indeed, death *is* imperceptible when defined as brain death, the loss of all brain activity and function. With zero or near zero functionality, the brain would have to produce a scientifically unexplainable kind of consciousness at or just before death by providing a perceived event (e_u) of unknown type and corresponding moment (m_u) that would somehow signal death. Given the supernatural nature of such an event and unless empirically shown otherwise, **death** is an imperceptible event, and the *Imperceptible Death* proposition is true.

Now, one must show that the implication ($\rightarrow$) is true. Given that one's consciousness is imperceptibly paused just before **death** and **death** is imperceptible, the period of timelessness before **death** continues forever (i.e., into the *After-Life* state in Figures 7.1 and 7.3 and the *After-Life* denoted in the NEC$_{FD}$). Thus with death, one never perceives a next conscious moment, one's consciousness remains paused in their final conscious moment, and this moment is essentially one's natural eternal consciousness. Therefore, the implication ($\rightarrow$) is true, and the NEC theory is "proven." ∎

To those with a firm belief in "nothingness" after death: indeed, *after* our last conscious moment, from a material perspective, we lose all awareness (perceive nothing new). Then we lose all memory and capacity for any non-supernatural awareness ever again. But from a psychological perspective—i.e., *the perspective of only what our minds perceive*—we perceive at some point in time t the last conscious moment of some experience, never perceiving it as our last. Then, for all time $> t$, we are unaware—i.e., *never perceive*—that the experience is over. Therefore, as deduced above, from our mind's perspective, the experience *at time t* is, as stated before, imperceptibly timeless and deceptively eternal. Admittedly, it is an illusion, but to the dying person, it is real.

The Issue of Memory Loss. Some will still object to the possibility of any eternal consciousness due to the loss of all memory in the **Severely Failing Brain** state. However, memory and remembering played no part in the "proof" of the PCT and NEC theories in Chapter 8. Nevertheless, below I specifically address this objection to the NEC theory even though it more generally applies to the issue of whether memory is necessary for preserving the present during all periods of timelessness before death. That is, the objection actually applies to the PCT theory.

Memory loss in the **Severely Failing Brain** state occurs at some point, though it would be imperceptible. (When it happens, I doubt anyone could say or think, "I just lost my memory.") And indeed, it could prevent remembering the last experience before timelessness *after awakening* as the first awake moment would instantly replace the last moment as the present. However, it cannot psychologically undo the present conscious moment and coexisting belief—i.e., self-awareness—that one's experience is still ongoing—i.e., that it has not ended—*before awakening*. Assuming an NDE is one's final experience, Figure 8.1 shows that *remembering* the last present moment of the NDE (e.g., m_{nde}) experienced just before *Timelessness* is not an issue. That is unless one wakes up and this moment is supplanted by a new present moment (e.g., m_r).

The Issue of Present Moment Loss. Now some, especially the more material-minded (and perhaps "computer-minded"), may want to claim that the loss of brain functioning in the **Severely Failing Brain** state or, if not that, surely death would wipe out not only memory but also the present moment from the brain. After all, is not this present moment, just like memory, stored somewhere

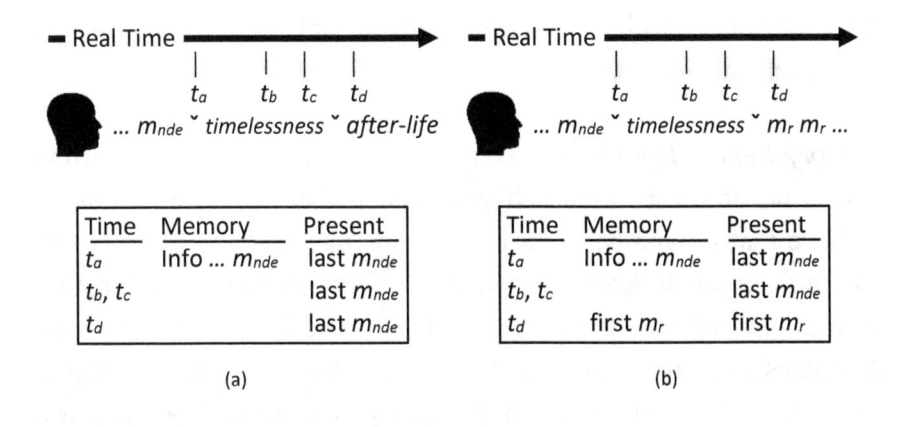

Figure 8.1. Two scenarios are depicted for NDEr P: (a) P dies and is dead at time t_d and (b) P recovers and perceives real moment m_r at t_d. In both scenarios, assume P enters the **Severely Failing Brain** state at t_a and at t_b loses all memory. A table for each scenario lists in column one the times t_a, t_b, t_c, and t_d. For each time, it shows in column two the moments indicated in the NEC notation that are in P's short-term "Memory" and in column three, the moment that P perceives as the "Present." Note that in (a), the loss of memory is irrelevant to the preservation of the present in the mind of P when this present (i.e., the last m_{nde}) is followed only by forever *timelessness*. In (b), memory loss is relevant but only because P wakes up and the present is supplanted by the first m_r.

within the brain? Well, it may very well be (perhaps in a set of brain cells one could label Present-Conscious-Moment), just like similar data is stored in a group of computer CPU registers (perhaps labelled Current-Computer-State). Unlike a computer, however, given human consciousness (still mysterious as it is), this moment has already been *felt* before death. It has already been "registered" in one's self-awareness. Though brain cells, like a computer's registers, are wiped out with death; however, it's too late because, as with any present moment, only another can change one's self-awareness.

Theory Versus Hypothesis. To close this section, I briefly return to the issue of theory versus hypothesis in the scientific context. I believe that a hypothesis based on principles and verifying observations can result in a theory when it offers insight and explanation into a new reality and can be validated. And I believe that a new hypothesis can be formulated based on a theory and, when validated, can result in a revision to the theory, a more general one, or a more specialized one. But no matter whether a hypothesis or theory, it must be empirically verified and its falsification must be possible to be scientific.

Chapter 9

Validity Via Testability
A Scientific Theory

In the previous chapter, I believe I've made a strong case for the validity of the NEC theory by showing that it can be logically deduced from empirical principles, which are supported by observation, experiment, or experience. However, in the previous chapter, I also indicated a deficiency in such a deduction. Specifically, it only provides a new "empirical truth," or empirical principle, provided the supporting principles complement one another without interference that can cause emergent consequences, like an explosion (as exemplified in the last chapter). Another deficiency with such a deduction is the possibility that some overlooked fact or principle exists that would invalidate the implication.

Verifiable and Falsifiable Before Death

These deficiencies, if they exist, must be able to be discovered by observation, experiment, or experience for any theory to attain the validity status of being deemed a scientific theory. Examples of scientific theories are Darwin's theory of evolution by natural selection and Einstein's special theory of relativity. They are scientific theories because they can be verified or falsified by testing. They have already been verified many times, so until falsified, they are considered valid theories. So, can the NEC theory also be so tested?

The short answer is yes. The next two paragraphs explain it in more detail. They summarize the remainder of this section, which makes the case in even more detail that the NEC theory can indeed be verified or falsified.

It is so because the NEC exists *before* death and does so psychologically—unlike any other kind of envisioned eternal consciousness or afterlife, all of which exist *after* death. The PCT theory has already been tested and verified zillions of times by everyday human experiences, like waking up from dreams. Moreover, the nearer to death are survivors who report on their last experiences, such as NDEs, but are unable to recall perceiving any moment of death, the more certain the NEC theory's validity. This is true because as brain functionality decreases to zero, the probability that a materially supported, unknown type of conscious moment exists that would wipe out one's awareness of their last moment as their present decreases to zero. The discovery of such a moment via focused research studies would falsify the NEC theory.

These studies may involve monitoring brain activity in dying patients,[12] interviews with near-death survivors, and further neuroscience research into the brain functionality required for perception in general and the production of the different types of conscious moments. I suggest and describe such a study in this chapter.

---

[12] Brain activity can be monitored using brain scanning tools like electroencephalography (EGE) and functional magnetic resonance imaging (fMRI). Activity in different parts of the brain indicate differing types of brain functionality. Memory access as well as dream and possible NDE activity have been studied using both tools (e.g., Chawla et al., 2018; Noh et al., 2018; Santangelo et al., 2018). Detecting and relating brain activity to functionality will likely only improve in the future.

Given advancements in brain monitoring technology and neuroscience that will continue, such studies should be possible, if not now, in the near future.

The PCT Theory: Testing

The PCT theory provides the primary support for the NEC theory. It is verified every time someone awakes from a period of timelessness, instantly surprised when their first awake moment is inconsistent with their last present one (as in waking up from a dream) or merely fascinated that they didn't know their last experience had ended (as in waking up from general anesthesia). Such *subjective* preservation of one's present during timelessness can be seen as no more than the imperceptible, temporary loss of the perception of any new moment to replace the present one within one's self-awareness. It can also be seen as a paused consciousness in timelessness (PCT).

But can the PCT theory be falsified? First, it would be falsified if individuals were waking up after a dream, NDE, or general anesthesia immediately aware that their dream or NDE had ended or they had passed out on the operating table, respectively. That is, they didn't feel the least bit surprised. But this has never been the case. Second, it would be falsified if neurological testing would show, via monitoring brain activity, that individuals waking up after a dream, NDE, or general anesthesia had immediately accessed their memory *before* feeling surprised by their first awake moment. If so, consciousness had not been paused but only regained by remembering.

In the last two years, I've had two opportunities to test the PCT theory with me as the guinea pig: two colonoscopies. With both, I received general anesthesia—specifically, put under "deep sedation" via Propofol. With both, I listened to the chatter between the medical people but purposely tried to remain alert to perceive the transitioning event into the timelessness that I knew awaited me.

Regarding the first colonoscopy, no luck, for the next thing I knew, I was in the recovery room. I was not surprised but fascinated that I never knew my last experience had ended, not a hint. Moreover, I didn't have to pause for one moment before being fascinated to remember that I had been on the operating table. My fascination then immediately turned into pleasure because the PCT theory had been verified.

Regarding the second colonoscopy, while again I tried to remain alert, I heard the rattle of wheels and sensed being rolled down a hallway. I thought something must have gone wrong with the equipment and they were taking me to another operating room. Nope, I was wrong. They wheeled me into the recovery room, and all was well.

The NEC Theory: Testing

But suppose I had died without ever waking up? How would I have ever known that I wasn't *currently* being "put under" for a colonoscopy? Hopefully, a pleasing dream or NDE would intervene to rescue me from this kind of NEC. But short of this hope, there is no way I would have ever known based on the NEC theory. Can this be verified or falsified by testing? The NEC theory is supported whenever the PCT theory is verified, but if the PCT theory is falsified, the NEC theory is falsified. So that's one way to falsify the NEC theory. The remainder of this section deals directly with other ways to verify or falsify the NEC theory via specific testing—i.e., testing to ensure a continuing paused consciousness as the dying person gets nearer and nearer to death.

In my colonoscopy experiences I described above, just maybe, *had I died*, my theory of a forever timelessness with a resultant

NEC was wrong. Perhaps, before death, I would have gotten some "new felt awareness"—i.e., some signal—that, for me, the present was no more and that there would be no more presents. Can studies be done to find such a signal? I claim this question is the same as asking, "Given the PCT theory, can the NEC theory be falsified?" I claim this because I believe that assuming a PCT, finding such a near-death signal is the only way to falsify the NEC theory.

So, I now show that psychological and neurological research studies of dying patients *near death* can verify or falsify the NEC theory. No testing is needed *after death* because any cognitive termination signal is impossible. I suggest studies that test the NEC theory and some of my underlying analyses.

This testing is possible because of the near certainty that a dying person never dies during any experience, even the NDE. Instead, as indicated by the timeless states preceding the event **death** in Figures 7.1 and 7.3 and by *Timelessness* in Figures 5.1 and the NEC$_{FD}$, a period of real time always follows the last conscious moment and precedes the event **death**. At least some of this period occurs within the **Severely Failing Brain** in Figure 7.3, which only ends after *all* brain activity has ceased. Detailed monitoring of electrical brain activity in dying rats (Borjigin et al. 2013) and people (Chawla et al. 2017) have supported the existence of this state as the time between the end of a sudden spike in brain activity, believed to be indicative of an NDE, and death. Such monitoring and its correlation with measures of brain functionality (*BF*) will only improve and become more commonplace with advances in neuroscience and technology.

To facilitate the description of my suggested research study, I again consider (as I did in the previous chapter) the possibility of a *perceived* unknown event (e_u) and corresponding conscious moment (m_u) that would occur very near death and somehow signal death. The NEC theory would be falsified by finding evidence of the e_u. If only a moment, it would somehow explicitly indicate to the dying person the onset of eternal timelessness or a before-life kind of nothingness, a "The End" claimed to be nonexistent in Chapter 1. The first or only m_u of the e_u would immediately replace a dying person's last moment from their self-awareness as the present moment—relegating their final experience to only the possibility of remembrance. But remembering would now be made impossible with the total loss of memory inherent in death.

Before I describe what is essentially a quest for e_u, I state below some reasons why this quest will probably be futile.

1. Any perception of death by a dying person would be technically premature as the perceiver would still be alive.
2. The perceiver, one's self, would still be present in the e_u, negating any true "nothingness." That is, the subjective preservation of self as present beyond death would still be maintained, and one would forever face the perception of death, a possibly gruesome prospect.
3. The e_u would be *perceived*—unlike all the other events besides death that transition one into timelessness and evidence our imperceptible loss of time (fall asleep, pass out, end dream, and end NDE).
4. Brain functionality (BF)—measured in terms of level and perhaps the location of brain activity—is rapidly decreasing as one approaches brain death, making the production and perception of any conscious moment increasingly impossible and thus scientifically unexplainable.
5. To the author's knowledge, no such e_u has ever been reported by near-death survivors and, if ever reported, would be logically contradictory to their having survived.

For these reasons, the existence of an e_u is not currently scientifically supported and, thus, like the traditionally envisioned afterlife, is supernatural. The moment of death is, after all, a physiological, not a psychological event. This, combined with verification of the CPT theory via much human experience, suggests the validity of the NEC theory until falsified by finding an e_u.

An analogy may prove helpful for those who still question the status of the NEC as a scientific theory based on the improbability of finding an e_u. The theory (or hypothesis)[13] of common descent states that all living organisms are descendants of a single ancestor. Biologist T. Ryan Gregory (2008) states:

> ... no reliable observation has ever been found to contradict the general notion of common descent. It should come as no surprise, then, that the scientific community at large has accepted evolutionary descent as a historical reality since Darwin's time and considers it among the most reliably established and fundamentally important facts in all of science. (p. 49)

Paul A M. van Dongen and Jo M. H. Vossen (1984), scholars in comparative and physiological psychology, state:

> The theory of common descent permits a large number of predictions of new results that would be improbable without evolution. For instance, ... (b) the observed order in fossils of new species discovered since Darwin's time could be predicted from the theory of common descent ... Such observations can be regarded as attempts to falsify the theory of common descent. We conclude that the theory of common descent is an easily falsifiable & often-tested & still-not-falsified theory, which is the strongest predicate a theory in an empirical science can obtain. (35)

Now, suppose someone finds a fossil that precisely matches an existing species that was assumed to have a place in the not-too-distant past on the evolutionary tree. Assume this first-of-its-kind fossil is dated very close to, or even earlier than, when life on earth

---

[13] The first article to be quoted on the concept of common descent considers it a hypothesis, the second a theory.

was thought to have begun (3.7 billion years ago). This finding contradicts the evolutionary order predicted by the theory of common descent and thereby falsifies the theory. Had this creature not evolved? Was it from outer space? Is finding such a fossil with respect to the theory of common descent like finding an m_u and e_u with respect to the NEC theory? To me, the former find would be less shocking than the latter.

Despite the improbability of finding an e_u, I offer below the prescription for a research study to show that the NEC theory can be tested. Given the variables and acronyms I use, those not interested in this prescription can skip it.

1. Brain functionality (*BF*) is closely monitored for many dying patients.

2. This monitoring and interviews with many <u>s</u>urvivors who were <u>n</u>ear <u>d</u>eath ($S_{nd}s$) reveal the following: the <u>s</u>urvivors who had an NDE ($S_{nde}s$); the signature brain activity identifying an NDE and its beginning and ending point; the <u>min</u>imum recorded *BF* for each S_{nd} ($S_{nd}minBF$); and the <u>min</u>imum *BF* recorded by any S_{nde} when NDE activity ceased ($minBF_{nde}$). Assuming a large enough sample size, this *BF* is the same as the minimum *BF* required for an NDE moment (m_{nde}) and corresponds to the below $minBF_{nde}$ event defined in Chapter 7. It thus identifies the beginning of the **Severely Failing Brain** state.

3. Neurological studies also reveal the minimum *BF* needed for the other types of conscious moments (m_r, m_i, m_h, and m_d). All of these *BF*s should be found greater than $minBF_{nde}$. If so, an e_u occurring within the **Severely Failing Brain** state (wherein *BF* < $minBF_{nde}$) cannot be perceived with ordinary consciousness.

(Note that if the minimum *BF* for a dream ($minBF_d$) is found to be less than $minBF_{nde}$, then the analysis and definitions related to the lifetime-in-eternity model would be called into question, but not necessarily the NEC theory.)

VALIDITY VIA TESTING: A SCIENTIFIC THEORY

4. Assume that neurological studies somehow precisely define the minimum *BF* that would for sure be required for any conscious perception, no matter the type. If this *BF* is found to be equal to *minBF$_{nde}$*, then an e_u is impossible, and *the NEC theory is verified*. In this case, there would be no need to interview S_{nd}s as described below.

5. All S_{nd}s having a $S_{nd}minBF$ < *minBF$_{nde}$*, meaning they had entered the **Severely Failing Brain** state, are carefully interviewed. If none report an e_u, *this finding would verify the NEC theory*.

6. Instead, if some of these S_{nd}s report an e_u, *this finding would falsify the NEC theory*. (It would suggest that many S_{nd}s could have perceived an e_u had they died). Furthermore, if it's found that all S_{nd}s report an e_u who had a $S_{nd}minBF$ < *maxBF$_u$* (for some *maxBF$_u$* < *minBF$_{nde}$*), *this finding would also falsify the NEC theory*. (Indeed, it would suggest that *maxBF$_u$* is the level of brain functionally below which every person who dies—i.e., eventually reaches *BF* = 0—would expect to perceive that they're dead.)

7. Once e_us have been reported, perhaps further research would reveal some signature brain activity that produces the e_u and is consistent with their reporting. It would support the falsification of the NEC theory based on the interviews.

It is important to note, however, that, as previously indicated, any e_u perceived by an S_{nd} would only signal *near*-nothingness to the dying person because it would include self. Moreover, it would be just a premonition—premature (since it occurred before death), wrong (since the person did not die), and highly unlikely for all the other reasons previously given.

Part III
Confronting the NEC Theory

There are two ways to be fooled. One is to believe what isn't true; the other is to refuse to believe what is true.
—Soren Kierkegaard, *Works of Love*, 1847

In Parts I and II, I've tried to help you develop a thorough understanding of the NEC theory by explaining the NEC and making a case for its "truth"—or, more accurately, its scientific reality. In this part, I focus on the NEC theory's impact and significance. In doing so, I address the psychological, philosophical, and religious aspects of accepting the theory (as one would the theory of evolution) and then dealing with it, perhaps even appreciating it.

Chapter 10

Accepting the Theory

All great truths begin as blasphemies.
—George Bernard Shaw

Previous chapters have been about understanding the NEC theory. However, understanding and accepting a new phenomenon, reality, or truth are mutually related. If a new truth is hard to grasp, it is certainly hard to accept. In Chapter 5, I discussed the difficulty of grasping and thereby accepting the NEC and the natural afterlife because of their illusionary nature. Yet, unfortunately, if a new truth, or reality, is hard to accept because of its controversial or undesirable impact, it is especially hard to grasp. And believe me, I've seen that the reality of the natural afterlife and the NEC seems "especially hard to grasp" for some. Why?

I blame this added difficulty on some general psychological impediments that stand in the way. If a new truth challenges orthodoxy or long-held personal beliefs, it's tough to accept. Moreover, it's even tougher to accept if one is heavily invested in the orthodoxy or beliefs. Furthermore, if a new truth can mean the risk of future unpleasantness (even more so *eternal* unpleasantness), it's also even tougher to accept. After I discovered the natural afterlife and later the NEC, I often wondered, "Why hasn't someone else discovered this before?" Based on my experiences with their acceptance, some of which I discuss below, I know that psychological impediments are a big part of why.

A Challenge to Orthodoxy, Big-time

The NEC theory indeed challenges centuries-old orthodoxy concerning death. The options for what to believe have essentially boiled down to two. When I die, 1) it will just be like before I was born or 2) I'll experience a supernatural afterlife wherein I'll retain some level of consciousness that includes my sense of self and time, the latter allowing for new experiences. In option 2, "supernatural" means not currently supported by science. Option 1 is often thought by its adherents to be backed by science, but it is not because, like option 2, it cannot be empirically verified or falsified. Option 2 most often stems from religious faith but need not. Some merely believe that a spiritual world awaits them that exists outside of our material one.

The NEC theory removes option one as a possibility but not option 2. It claims a default after-life, possibly an etna, that replaces option one yet doesn't rule out the possibility of an option 2 type of afterlife overriding it. Unlike option 1, the NEC after-life includes one's sense of self. Unlike option 2, it does not include one's sense of time (i.e., of any passage of time). Though this sense is present for a time in the etna, it is imperceptibly lost in the natural afterlife. Unlike both options, the NEC is scientifically supported.

Thus, the NEC theory, especially in denying option one, significantly "upsets the applecart." I dare say it does so as much as other earth-shattering ideas that have challenged orthodoxy throughout history. Examples are: the earth is not flat but spherical, it is not the center of the universe, the sun does not orbit the earth but vice versa, the continents are drifting, and humankind has evolved. I believe that, like these ideas, the NEC theory, though challenging for many to accept at first, will become widely accepted in the future.

George Bernard Shaw (2009) wrote in a playlet, "All great truths begin as blasphemies," and German philosopher Arthur Schopenhauer is quoted as stating, "All truth passes through three stages. First, it is ridiculed. Second, it is violently opposed. Third, it is accepted as being self-evident" (The Age of Ideas n.d.). The NEC theory has been seen as blasphemy. It and I have been ridiculed and strenuously opposed—though, thankfully, not yet violently opposed. In opposition, I have encountered "religiously" zealous beliefs in option 1 that likely can't be surpassed by any such beliefs in option 2.

Soon after publishing my first article (Ehlmann 2013a), I thought I would open it up for public discussion with a couple of posts on the social media site Reddit (https://www.reddit.com/). Big mistake! It and I immediately became the target of ridicule. My mere claim that the theory of a natural afterlife was *consistent with science* was called "Bullshit" by one commenter. The "whole article" was called "junk science" by another. Being *only* a "retired computer scientist," I was accused by still another of having "neither science nor expertise." And one commenter stated that the referenced article (Ehlmann 2013a) "made my brain throw up." I had made my posts under the categories of "Religion" and "DebateReligion," where I later learned via the internet that much of the discourse was dominated by atheists, who often would swarm over anyone expressing any theist or afterlife belief.

I should point out that over the past few years, such ridicule has significantly subsided with the publishing of scholarly articles on the natural afterlife and the NEC. Also, thankfully, the natural afterlife and NEC theory have not yet been "violently opposed." However, as of this writing, they are "self-evident" to relatively few. A cautious guess would be fewer than one hundred thousand.

A Challenge to Publish

Seemingly, these few do not include the journal editors and reviewers responsible for rejecting two of my articles before being finally accepted by another journal. These are my theory of a natural afterlife article (Ehlmann 2016) and my NEC theory article (Ehlmann 2020). From my first submission to acceptance, I endured eight rejections over 25 months for the 2016 article and eighteen over almost the same length of time for my 2020 article. These journal submissions are listed in Table 10.1 for the 2016 article and Table 10.2 for the 2020 article in the order submitted. For each journal submission, I summarize the kind of response I received. None of the responding editors or reviewers are identified, with two exceptions.

Although listing and discussing one's article rejections is very unusual, my objectives in doing so are:

- To show the ordeal one can face in trying to publish a discovery that challenges orthodoxy in a scholarly journal.

- To show how a relatively straightforward concept can sometimes be so difficult to grasp and accept by experts in the related fields. Here, the concept is that you will die never knowing your final experience is over (which I hope most readers have grasped by now), and the experts are numerous psychology and philosophy scholars. Is this because the concept is unorthodox? Because of its elusive essence? Perhaps some combination of both? Or might there be other issues in play?

- To show the number of psychology and philosophy scholars who have reviewed my theories and have not offered any legitimate objections or pointed out any flaws. The only objections have come from those who did not grasp the theories, as was evident from their comments.

- To encourage others, especially young scholars, to not give up on publishing their ideas or discoveries too soon. If you believe in them, go for it and be tenacious.

These objectives, I believe, can be accomplished by a quick scan of the tables on your part and some elaboration on my part.

Table 10.1
Submissions for the 2016 Theory of a Natural Afterlife Article

#	Journal - Summary of Response
1	*Journal of Near-Death Studies* – Reviewer #1 felt many aspects of NDEs (all irrelevant to the theory) were not discussed. #2 felt some statements were not supported by references and needed clarification. Resubmission was doomed when #3 felt that an NDE ending in death was not an NDE as it occurs after death.
2	*Mortality* – After five months, rejected based on two reviewers. #1 failed to grasp the theory and claimed I had made assumptions that I did not. #2 felt the theory was based too much on unsupported claims instead of arguments and evidence."
3	*eLife* – The article "makes interesting reading" but was judged not "suitable for *eLife* precisely because it doesn't provide data and their analyses."
4	*Death Studies* – The reviewer enjoyed reading the article but felt it is simply too speculative to be considered for publication in *Death Studies*."
5	*International Journal for Philosophy of Religion* – I was told that reviewers thought the article "did not sufficiently advance discussions about the afterlife." No further comments were given.
6	*Ergo* – Reviewer failed to grasp the theory, indicating that I failed to show that "a conscious life … can be sustained by something other than … body and brain."
7	*Cosmos and History* – 3.5 mos. for review. A single reviewer never grasped the natural afterlife's essence and demanded a total rewrite. Was resubmitted. After over 7 mos. (inquiries were unanswered), rejected with no additional feedback.
8	*Journal of Scientific Exploration* – Again, a single reviewer never grasped the natural afterlife's essence, misconstrued statements, and was even hostile. I felt that he considered the natural afterlife hostile to his view of an afterlife.
9	*Journal of Consciousness Exploration and Research* - Finally, an editor who truly grasped the natural afterlife's essence! He stated, "so pleased … with your unique concept of a timeless 'natural afterlife' that is not 'after' … since it's timeless."

In Table 10.1, when I indicate a reviewer did not grasp the essence, I mean they didn't understand the timeless and relativeness nature of the natural afterlife. Because of this, they would just continue to essentially argue that "when you're dead, you can't experience anything," essentially Hypothesis 1 in Chapter 4.

I must admit, however, that my explanations of the natural afterlife may not have been as good in my earlier submissions as in my later ones. However, on my ninth submission, I *finally* found an open-minded editor who genuinely understood and appreciated the theory of a natural afterlife. I felt exonerated, elated, and extremely relieved. And I knew he understood the afterlife's timeless and relativistic essence when he stated in an email to me what I quoted in Table 10.1 and stated in a later email:

> I read ... about how time comes to a standstill on the edge of an event horizon in a black hole for any possible observer, so any spaceship would appear frozen in time forever at that edge (like a corpse). However, for *anyone on that ship*, time would not stop and they would continue plummeting into the unknown depths of the Black Hole, beyond light, beyond time, beyond substance. For some reason that made me think of your theory, as I understand it ... Something timeless "continues" beyond the frozen time of the corpse. (G. M. Nixon, email, November 26, 2016)

In the first sentence of this section, I stated "Seemingly" regarding the rejections of my article by journal editors and reviewers because, as Table 10.2 shows, it seemed to be the article, not the NEC theory, that was being rejected. In just one case, the theory was rejected. So as rejections continued, I gained more confidence in the theory as more psychology and philosophy scholars reviewed it without challenging it. Only two did so, both from the same journal (#16). But I dismissed their objections as

Table 10.2
Submissions for the 2020 NEC Theory Article

#	Journal - Summary of Response
1	*Timing and Time Perception* – The subject is outside the journal's scope. Recommend you try another journal.
2	*Perspectives on Psychological Science* - Too metaphysical. No hard evidence for the claims. **Recommend you submit to a journal specializing in consciousness.**
3	*Psychological Inquiry* - An interesting article, but we can only accept a very limited number of articles. I look forward to its publication elsewhere.
4	*Cognitive Science* – The article doesn't link to the work we publish or to empirical evidence. **Recommend a philosophical journal or one devoted to consciousness** (e.g., *Consciousness and Cognition* or *Frontiers in Consciousness Research*).
5	*Consciousness and Cognition* – The article doesn't fit well with the type of articles we publish. **Recommend you try** the *Journal of Consciousness Studies* (see #16).
6	*Philosophical Psychology* - (pre-submission inquiry) Publication is possible, but **first, try submitting to journals dealing more with phenomenology:** *Phenomenology and the Cognitive Sciences* (see #10) and *Phenomenology and Mind*.
7	*Frontiers in Psychology, Theoretical and Philosophical Psychology* – The article does not meet the journal's standards of rigor.
8	*Frontiers in Psychology, Cognition* - Does not meet the journal's standards of rigor. The claims being made cannot, in principle, be tested.
9	*Frontiers in Psychology, Consciousness Research* - Does not meet the journal's standards of rigor. More specifically, the theory is not empirically testable and not based on objective science. (Just another of *Frontiers* form letters.)
10	*Phenomenology and the Cognitive Sciences* - Looks very interesting but seems overly speculative. **Recommend submitting it to a philosophy journal.**
11	*PLOS* - The article is not a strong candidate for publication. **Recommend submitting it to a psychology journal.**
12	*Cognition* -The topics covered are outside the scope of the journal. **Recommend submitting the article to a religion or philosophy journal.**
13	*Cognitive Psychology* - Theory was not evaluated by methods of experimental psychology. Read with great interest. Unusual and provocative. Seems more philosophical. **Recommend** *Perspectives on Psychological Science* (See #2)
14	*Journal of Theoretical and Philosophical Psychology* - The article may be more appropriate for another journal.
15	*Religion, Brain, and Behavior* - (pre-submission inquiry) Your article would be better suited for another journal.
16	*Journal of Consciousness Studies* - Rejected based on two reviews. Reviewer #1 believed that NDEs occur *after* death. #2 stated that nothing can be timeless and eternal, failing to grasp the NEC's relativity. (So I had no chance.)
17	*Ergo* - Submission is not accepted for publication. The handling editor did not provide any feedback.
18	*Philosophers Imprint* - I have decided not to pursue the article for publication.
19	*The Journal of Mind and Behavior* – "WOW! I'm a bit speechless." First conditionally accepted, then later **Accepted**!

one would not accept that NDEs occur before death (as did one reviewer discussed in Table 10.1), and the other that something could be "timelessly eternal." Most of the editors, twelve of eighteen, encouraged me to submit my article to a more suitable journal.

So, as the process went on, I just worked harder to improve my cover letter and article. And sure enough, eventually, once again, I felt exonerated, elated, and extremely relieved. However, this time it was the *nineteenth* submission, and again I believe it was an open-minded editor that finally made the difference.

Some psychology journals listed in Table 10.2 rejected the article because experimental results were not given to verify the theory. Though the article deduces the theory from established, empirically supported psychological principles and describes how it could be tested, that was not enough. One editor, after I pleaded for more specific feedback, since I had gotten almost none from my prior submissions, graciously replied with the comment below—which for me, was enlightening:

> I think the problem is that psychology is an empirical discipline. We want theories that explain objectively observable facts. There are lots of well-established cognitive principles that can be combined to make new cognitive theories. But psychologists want more than the theory. They want the theory to be tested. ... For a psychology journal, the issue isn't whether your reasoning is flawed. The main issue is whether your theory is tested using the methods of experimental psychology. It isn't, so that takes it off the table. ... Indeed, those are the standards I've had to live up to throughout my career. (G. D. Logan, email, December 11, 2018)

Given such a mindset—seemingly, a need for immediate gratification regarding testing—I could see why no psychologist had discovered the NEC. By "the problem" (in the first line of the quote), I knew the editor meant the lack of NEC theory testing and agreed the article could better address the issue of testing, but I also thought part of "the problem" was with psychology. I responded to the editor with the following:

> Logical deduction is an extremely valuable part of critical thinking. It, like a mind, "is a terrible thing to waste." Computer science, mathematics, logic, physics, and philosophy—in decreasing order given, the major disciplines in my background—very much value deduction. ... obvious implications, when identified, should be of great interest rather than readily dismissed simply because immediate testing is lacking. This should be especially true when an implication contradicts a discipline's orthodox view that itself is an implication that lacks testing.

I then pointed out (as in Chapter 4) how most psychology textbooks, in defining the mind as a product of the brain and consciousness as only a *dynamic* process of the brain, clearly imply the orthodox view that when the brain dies, so must consciousness. But *this* obvious implication has not been tested, nor can it be.

Though I admit this view has not been made explicit by psychology, it has been left implicitly dangling in front of students for decades, some of whom become future instructors. This situation has been the case despite psychology's cognitive principles (as given in Chapter 4) contradicting it. They imply that consciousness becomes *static* with death (i.e., paused in a moment). Such contradictory implications of major interdisciplinary significance should not be so readily just "taken off the table" by psychology when they are brought to light.

I went on to state:

> Some of our greatest scientific theories were very controversial when first published and, important to this discussion, likely did not meet the rigorous testing standards of psychology as you've stated. Yet, they generated much in-

terest and experimentation within their disciplines. The special theory of relativity and the theory of evolution by natural selection immediately come to mind. I'm glad that Einstein and Darwin didn't have to meet psychology's standards.

Note that Einstein's theory was deduced via thought experiments and formalized by mathematics. Darwin's theory was deduced via observations. Only later were both verified by more focused and formal testing. I used thought experiments (e.g., thinking about not waking up from a dream) and observations (e.g., experiencing and observing transitions to and from periods of timelessness) to deduce the NEC theory. I formalized it with a model that used a mathematical-like notation involving variables and operators (represented by tracks, symbols, and implicit equivalences). See Chapter 8.

Luckily, I finally found a psychology journal that appreciated deduction and theorization. In fact, its scope description stated: "Please note: JMB does not typically publish empirical research." Hallelujah!

After my experience in trying to get my 2020 article published, I began to suspect possible, unstated reasons for my article's rejections. Many journal editors had not addressed the substance of the NEC theory, not even the testing issue. They merely stated the article was outside their scope—when it seemed well within, according to their website. I was not a psychology scholar and had no record of psychology publications. So, a related reason may have been the "not discovered here" syndrome, where "here" was the community of psychology and cognitive science scholars. Also, my article's multi-disciplinary nature was problematic. The principles were psychological, the analysis employed computer science tools, and the implications of the theory were philosophical and religious. Also, journals are hesitant to risk their reputation. By accepting an article, they're giving it their "stamp of approval." So, why accept an article with an author like me that would "rock the boat," impact many people's beliefs, and thus be very controversial? Just let another journal take the risk.

Psychological and Theory-Specific Impediments

While one or more of these reasons may have been impediments that kept journals from publishing the NEC theory, more personal impediments have and will likely continue to keep individuals from accepting it. Generally speaking, there are psychological reasons for individuals not to want to accept anything new that challenges orthodoxy. First, one does not like to admit they've been wrong for many years. Moreover, one does not like being forced to reexamine and reformulate other beliefs and viewpoints stemming from their orthodox ones. And finally, one may feel their reputation may be tarnished if it has been heavily invested in public pronouncements or publications of beliefs and viewpoints that the new idea would render wrong or outdated. Thus, a powerful bias exists for individuals to want to cling to old orthodoxies rather than come to grips with new realities.

Now add to these psychological impediments reasons for certain individuals not to want to accept, not just any new theory, but specifically, the NEC theory. First and foremost, this theory is often immediately seen as an affront to one's religious or antireligious beliefs. For atheists, the mere mention of the possibility of an afterlife is often instantly viewed as blasphemy. As indicated before, the angriest reactions to the NEC and natural afterlife have come from atheists on social media sites. Most of them, I am sure, had either not bothered to read a related article I referenced or just quickly scanned it. For the religious, the first mention of a *natural* afterlife is often instantly viewed as *the* afterlife being claimed as the replacement for the one provided by God.

Second, regardless of any strong beliefs about the afterlife, for those who are very scientifically minded (perhaps including the journal editors and reviewers discussed above), barriers to acceptance immediately arise upon simply seeing the terms *natural afterlife* or *natural eternal consciousness*. Given the old orthodoxy, these terms are oxymorons.

Third, aspects of the NEC and natural afterlife present still more impediments toward acceptance because of the kind of afterlife it offers. First, the NEC is timeless, whether perceived as an afterlife or not. Nothing happens! One will not be able to continue their relationship with their loved ones or perhaps play the golf they enjoy. Also, its content may be unpleasant, maybe even downright hellish. As mentioned in Chapter 6, one study of NDErs concluded that the percentage of *distressing NDEs* (*dNDEs*) is in the middle to high teens and added that dNDEs are likely underreported (Bush 2009, 81; IANDS 2017). Worse yet, any unpleasantness will be eternal since the NEC is eternal. And, since the content of dreams and NDEs seem indeterminant, so does the content of the NEC and natural afterlife. The risk and the seeming randomness of "what dreams may come" with death (as Hamlet wondered) can be terrifying.

The next chapter addresses some of these impediments to acceptance, hopefully providing some enlightenment on them and easing some fears. But before getting into "Dealing with the Theory," I give examples of nonacceptance and acceptance by some individuals.

An Example of Nonacceptance. Below is a dialogue I had in 2014 with an individual on Reddit who shall remain anonymous. They had responded to a question I had posted to gauge acceptance of my theory of a natural afterlife. Their comments made it evident to me that they likely didn't believe in an afterlife, much less a forever blissful moment.

ACCEPTING THE THEORY

I think the dialogue shows the difficulty of understanding the natural afterlife when one does not *want* to accept it. Their problem is with its imperceptibly timeless essence, and I believe their lack of acceptance is due to their belief in a riskless before-life kind of nothingness upon death. The article I reference in my paragraph elaborating on the posted question, given below, is an overview article that I had posted on the internet. It is titled "Your Natural Afterlife: the Non-Supernatural Alternative to Nothingness" (Ehlmann 2013b).

Remember this person's opinion on a "forever blissful moment" because it is quite the opposite of that expressed by a psychology scholar, which I give in the final chapter.

> **Question:** Can you envision and appreciate an afterlife that is, for you, an everlasting, extremely blissful moment?
>
> By "moment" I mean it's timeless (i.e., nothing more happens). However, it encompasses the sights, sounds, smells, and all of your associated feelings present at a particular point in time. These feelings may include the feeling that similar moments are now your future. The possibility of such a dream-based afterlife is presented in "Your Natural Afterlife: the Non-Supernatural Alternative to Nothingness" and related articles.
>
> **Responder:** Can I envision one? Of course. But would I appreciate it? No, god no. One never-ending moment of elation would be the equivalent of hell for me. To live is my greatest joy, all the things I feel, the despair, the fury, the elation, all these things are what make life worth living for me. One solitary emotion forever would not be living, it would be eternal torment. The worst part is, I wouldn't even be able to feel that pain.

Me: A "moment of elation" cannot be *turned into* a "hell" or "eternal torment." There is no time for that since the moment is timeless.

Responder: I know. I'm saying that being unable to experience anything else would be the equivalent of hell for me. For me, life is not the pursuit of happiness; it is the pursuit of all experiences. Therefore, an eternal moment of elation is but an empty shell of an existence, and one not worth having. To be without suffering is suffering in [and] of itself.

Me: "To be without suffering is suffering in of itself"? Really? And even for just a moment?

Responder: What I mean is a life of happiness without sadness and anger, is empty. Emptiness is suffering. And no, you speak of an eternal moment. An eternal moment is still an eternity. Feeling one thing for all eternity, even if I do not notice any passage of time, is still the most disgusting thing I could imagine. I would rather have the void. No consciousness is better than a forced consciousness.

Maybe if it wasn't described as eternal bliss, but instead as eternal consciousness, I could appreciate it. But eternal happiness? That's a fool's dream. Take a meth addict, all they want is to feel that high forever, to be eternally happy. Sounds similar, doesn't it?

Me: If you are happy in the moment and "do not notice any passage of time," I fail to see how this can be even mildly disgusting. Also, the moment is not induced by any artificial means (i.e., drugs) or "forced" but rather by nature. And btw, it doesn't have to be (and should not be!) something for which one lives their life. After all, it's only a possibility, maybe a little icing on the cake.

Evidence of Acceptance Despite Impediments

I close this chapter on a positive note with some examples of positive feedback that I've received on the natural afterlife and NEC. Despite all of the impediments to their acceptance, somehow, some individuals were able to overcome them. Three of the quotes below are the same as those given in the Prologue.

Gregory M. Nixon—philosophy and consciousness scholar, editor, and writer—after reviewing my Ehlmann (2016) article submission, stated:

> I've received a fair number of papers dealing with the NDE and—in spite of the unique direction you've taken—yours is by far the most comprehensive, the most fair-minded, and, frankly, the most extraordinary ….

About the same article, Jeffrey Long MD, the author of Long (2010), stated in an email, "I hope your article is published because it is a fascinating new line of thinking about the afterlife. I see no flaws in my brief review." (J. Long, email, 2016)

The same article was cited in the YouTube video "10 Theories About the Afterlife" (Alltime10s 2018). In the video, the theory of a natural afterlife gained recognition as theory #5 (at 4:33) and garnered some positive comments. Note that the problem of testing raised in the video was later addressed in both my Ehlmann (2020) and Ehlmann (2022) articles. Also, from the video, one might get the impression that the natural afterlife would be like a "Ground Hog Day" experience (as in the movie). It's not. The dying person senses no repetition of their last moment.

After reviewing my submission of the 2020 article, the journal editor, Raymond C. Russ, exclaimed: "Wow! I'm a bit speechless! … my 'wow' pertained to the writing and topic, everything."

In October 2020, I got an email from a reader of my articles who still distinctly remembers what he called a "vivid dream" but was likely an NDE that he had "unconscious ... as a kid" (J. Weiskel, email, October 31, 2020). He suggested I give a TED Talk because he stated, "you are the only person whom I feel understands the concept of an eternal, personal afterlife in a personal timeless (and out of time) state. The brick wall people hit with 'you can't dream if your brain is dead' would be nice to see knocked down."

Lastly, Figure 10.1 gives the results as of November 2022 of a running Survey at the end of an article I posted on *HubPages* in November 2013. The article is titled "Your Natural Afterlife: The Non-supernatural Alternative to Nothingness" (Ehlmann 2013b). As can be seen, a large majority of readers thought the natural afterlife was possible after reading the article. The most significant result is the article's impact on those who believed they would experience nothing after death or didn't know what they would experience.

ACCEPTING THE THEORY

What did you believe you would experience after death prior to reading this article?
- ☐ 32% A) Some type of supernatural afterlife
- ■ 33% B) Nothing
- ■ 35% C) Don't know

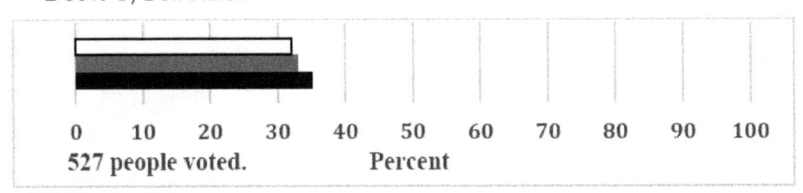

527 people voted.   Percent

If you chose A above, do you believe the natural afterlife is possible after reading this article?
- ☐ 73% A) Yes
- ■ 27% B) No

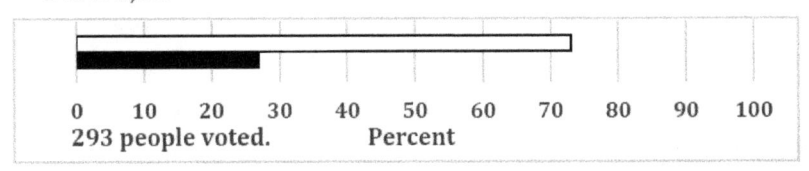

293 people voted.   Percent

If you chose B above, do you believe the natural afterlife is possible after reading this article?
- ☐ 64% A) Yes
- ■ 36% B) No

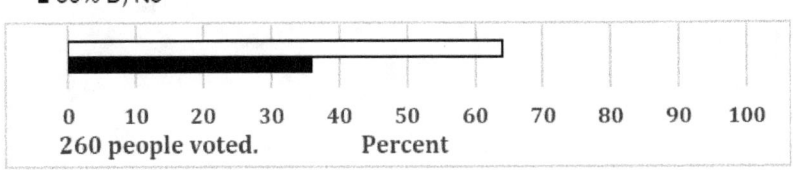

260 people voted.   Percent

If you chose C above, do you believe the natural afterlife is possible after reading this article?
- ☐ 74% A) Yes
- ■ 26% B) No

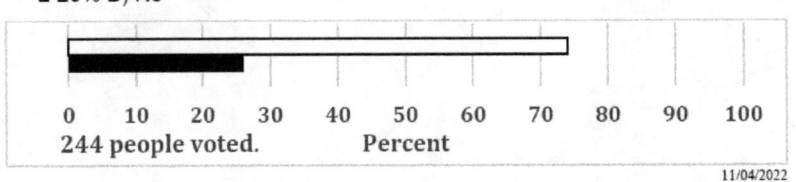

244 people voted.   Percent

11/04/2022

Figure 10.1. Survey on the natural afterlife. (Ehlmann 2013b)

Chapter 11

Dealing With the Theory
Philosophical and Religious Viewpoints

The day which we fear as our last is but the birthday of eternity.
—Lucius Annaeus Seneca, "De Brevitate Vitae" (ca. 48 C.E.)

If one cannot deal with a new truth, it is hard to accept. However, it can be hard to deal with, even if one can accept it. This can be especially true with the NEC theory. So, how does one deal with this theory?

Overcoming Prior Expectations, Beliefs, and Biases

To begin, how do you deal with the fact that the NEC is timeless if you expect an eternal, perfect afterlife filled with many pleasurable activities? First, as pointed out in Chapter 6, you must realize that an activity-filled, thus time-perceiving, infinite perfect afterlife that allows one to have the freedom to make decisions is illogical. And if illogical, it's impossible.

But some will say, "But with God, nothing is impossible." implying that God can make even the illogical possible. If you believe this, you must also believe in a God who can make a stone so large that he could not roll it up a hill or allow you free will but ensure no decision you make is less than perfect. That is, you must believe in a God who makes contradictory statements true. Regardless of whether an illogical afterlife is or is not possible, I point out again that the NEC theory does not preclude such an afterlife. It only claims that it would have to override the NEC.

Second, you must realize that a time-perceiving afterlife is unnecessary to provide the utmost eternal happiness, as argued in Chapter 6. Briefly restated here, this is because once you've achieved utmost happiness via previous events, more events cannot result in more happiness but only risk less. This fact was the second basis for the eta (eventually timeless afterlife) principle, which I restate below, the first being the illogicalness of the time-perceiving eternal, perfect afterlife.

Any afterlife that is perfect—i.e., provides utmost eternal happiness—must be an underline{e}ventually underline{t}imeless underline{a}fterlife (eta).

Fortunately, the etna is an eta. Activities can occur. They do so before death, but the dying person doesn't know this. They believe these activities are part of their afterlife. For example, activities with loved ones can occur, whether alive or dead. As mentioned in Chapter 6, a study found that perceptions of meeting deceased loved ones within ELDVs were prevalent as participants approached death (Kerr et al. 2014, Abstract). With the etna, these loved ones can be *timelessly* with you forever. Unlike any other afterlife known to me, the etna allows a progression of activities to climax into a glorious moment of maximum happiness and then be forever frozen in one's consciousness.

In the last sentence, change glorious to "awful" and "happiness" to "sadness" or "distress." "Ay, there's the rub," as Hamlet had feared. How does one deal with this most horrendous possibility? This possibility may be especially unsettling for those who do not believe in hell. Before discussing it more, however, I discuss the reactions to the NEC theory I got from two philosophers, P2 and P3, and also indicate my religious leanings. (I discussed philosopher P1's reaction in Chapter 5.)

Both P2 and P3 are acknowledged agnostic atheists. By "agnostic," I mean *Merriam-Webster*'s first definition: "a person who holds the view that any ultimate reality (such as God) is unknown and probably unknowable."

P2 stated that the theory was most likely valid because he could not find any flaws, but admitted that he was always hoping it was not as he read my NEC theory article (Ehlmann 2020). He said that he was bothered by the uncertainty of having a near-death dream or NDE and, if he had one, what its content would be. To get this feedback, I had to ask him what he thought of the article after much time had passed since I gave him a copy because he had expressed an interest in reading it (given its general subject matter) and promised to provide me with feedback. I have had similar experiences with others. Most often, though, I never bothered to follow up as I suspected the article may have left the person bewildered, perhaps now uncertain about their after-life beliefs, and not particularly ready or anxious to discuss them with me.

Philosopher P3, also of Wikipedia fame, like P1, accepted that the NEC theory was very likely valid. However, he dismissed it as of no consequence for two reasons.

First, the natural afterlife is undesirable because it is timeless. He thought that if one was going to believe in an afterlife, which he did not, it should be one that provided new experiences. My reaction to this was basically: So what? If you accept its reality, even its possibility, the natural afterlife "is what it is." What one then thinks would be a better afterlife is irrelevant. One must deal with what is, not what one wishes.

Second, he stated that the natural afterlife is delusional (i.e., just an illusion) and philosophers "do not deal with illusions," only reality. My reply essentially was: But as an illusion—although the setting, characters, and prior plot may not be real—it *is* a reality just as much as the many other illusions that our minds conjure up—e.g., rainbows or the solidity of objects. And besides, the feelings and emotions aroused are undeniably real and, for the dying person, become eternal.

If I had focused on the etna before my discussion with P3, I could have pointed out to him that the etna can be an experience comprised of many new activities. Also, although the eternity of the etna is delusional, these activities are just as real *to the dying person* as those within any other experience in life, no matter the type—awake, dream, or NDE. The only difference is that they are followed by eternal timelessness instead of temporary timelessness.

Given these reasons were P3's only objections to the NEC theory, I felt very pleased with his feedback. After reading Lanza (2009), I had come to appreciate that the world as we know it, even when awake and alert, is not what is actually out there. Rather, *this world is what our minds perceive*—filtered and transformed by our sense organs from matter and energy, supplemented and influenced by our stored memories, rendered into discrete conscious moments, and then perhaps interpreted yet again by our prejudices. In the case of ELDVs and NDEs, the "material," or physical, is imperceptibly formed from previously stored memories. Though again, some believe it may come from or at least be influenced by another source.

I felt that P3, though accepting the NEC theory, was grasping for reasons to dismiss it so as not to have to deal with it. Perhaps, I suspected, this was because P3 had strongly believed for decades that there was no afterlife, thinking any afterlife had to be supernatural, and had written many scholarly publications that promoted and assumed this belief. For those believing that death guarantees a before-life kind of nothingness, especially those heavily invested in this belief, the NEC theory requires some major and unwelcomed recalibration.

Where I'm Coming From

> *Science without religion is lame, religion without science is blind.*
> —Albert Einstein

> *Almost the whole world is asleep ... only a few people are awake, and they live in a state of constant, total amazement.*
> —"Joe Versus the Volcano," the movie (1990)

I like to think of myself as being one of the awake. In the above, one of my favorite sayings, I interpret "awake" as knowing what science has to tell us about our world, being open-minded about what it cannot tell us, and knowing which is which. Obviously, one cannot be knowledgeable about all of science, but what is vital to being "awake" is to have general knowledge about those aspects of science that are relevant to one's fundamental beliefs, religious and philosophical, and have such beliefs be consistent with science. Then, I believe one cannot help but "live in a state of constant, total amazement" (well, at least on many occasions).

Before I continue to address dealing with the NEC, I think it only fair to disclose my religious and philosophical beliefs—which to my knowledge, are consistent with science. But before I do, I preface my disclosure with another dose of external reality and two more quotations, which I often think of when pondering my religious beliefs and those of others.

First are the quotations, one from the Bible and one from a marketing agency:

> [1] Then the Lord answered Job out of the whirlwind: [2] "Who is this that darkens counsel by words without knowledge? ... [4] Where were you when I laid the foundation of the earth? Tell me, if you have understanding. [5] Who determined its measurements—surely, you know! Or who stretched the line upon it? [6] On what were its bases sunk, or who laid its cornerstone, [7] when the morning stars sang together, and all the sons of God shouted for joy? (RSV, Job 38:1-7)

> A mind is a terrible thing to waste. (slogan, *United Negro College Fund*, Young & Rubicam, 1972)

These two quotes may seem at odds. In the first, God is mocking Job for using his limited mind to dare question "the Lord" as to the reasons for his sufferings. I believe these Bible verses are explained very well in the essay "The Problem of Suffering," which is in a book series that was the basis of a course on the Bible that I attended in the late 1970s (Fretheim & Beekmann 1972).

> God countered [Job] with a series of questions, all of which point to the severe limits of man and his ability to comprehend the world of which he is a part. God exposed the naïveté of both Job and his friends in their assumption that immediately behind each of man's problems there is an easy explanation of divine intention. The speeches point to the absolute marvelousness and ultimate incomprehensibility of God's management of the world. They serve to force man back into a recognition of his limitations in relationship to God. (155)

By pointing out to Job the limitations of his knowledge and understanding—as in "Who is this ... without knowledge?" and "Tell me, if you have understanding."—God is implying their importance. That is, God is recognizing the ability of humans to gain knowledge and understanding. This acknowledgment shouldn't be surprising because, supposedly, it was God who gave humans a mind.

And if true, I believe God expects humans to use it, not waste it, which is consistent with the second quotation above. So, I should use my mind to form my religious and philosophical beliefs, even given its limitations regarding God and my existence in this universe. This is especially true since these beliefs, more so than any others, strongly affect how I live and treat others.

So I am a student of religion just like I am of science. I don't simply assume the beliefs that I was brought up with or take the word of religious leaders—who must be concerned with upholding tradition, being careful not to ruffle feathers (i.e., sensitivities) within their flock, and keeping their position. Just as I've studied textbooks and articles on scientific research written by scholars, I've likewise studied biblical and religious research—and not just publications from scholars at seminaries but also from those at secular colleges and universities because they are vast and offer a wealth of knowledge. The books authored by New Testament scholar Bart D. Ehrman (e.g., 2014, 2020) are prime examples.

Figure 11.1 is an image created by the Hubble Space Telescope of about 1/32,000,000 of the sky. Only two of the specks of light are stars in our Milky Way galaxy. The other 5,500 specks that can be counted are galaxies—each containing, on average, about 100,000,000,000 stars. Assuming roughly five planets per star system (we have eight in our solar system), how many planets might there be in the universe? Based on this image (Cink 2021):

$$5,500 \times 100,000,000,000 \times 5 \times 32,000,000 = 8.8 \times 10^{20}$$

That's 880,000,000,000,000,000,000 planets!

Just imagine how many beings might live on these planets with about the same or more human intelligence. How many believe in a God? Perhaps have a religious faith like yours? Given your faith's earth-centric aspects, if any, how many could you convert?

Figure 11.1. The Hubble XDF (eXtreme Deep Field) Image having a field of view covering 1/32,000,000 of the sky. Only two specks of light are stars; the others are all galaxies. (NASA 2012)

Now having established a cosmic perspective and my belief in fully utilizing one's God-given mind in forming one's religious beliefs, I now divulge mine. Though born and raised a Missouri Synod Lutheran, I now see myself as an agnostic theist and very liberal-minded Christian. By the former, I mean that I *believe* God exists but cannot claim that I *know* God exists (Cline 2019, Key Takeaways). Regarding the latter, my Christianity has evolved from the conservative theology I was taught as a child and teen—

i.e., the inerrancy of the Bible and the dogma of the Christian creeds—by becoming more educated about science and biblical scholarship. (Given the wealth of such scholarship, I marvel that so many Christian fundamentalists have not so evolved.)

However, I still value my Christian upbringing because it was the Bible—the commandments and especially the teachings of Christ in parables and the Sermon on the Mount (Matt. 5-7)—that gave me my moral compass and an unachievably high standard that I *strive* to live by. Moreover, parts of the Bible, along with similarly inspired writings over the ages, continue to challenge me to be more Godlike, as was exemplified by Christ. And I still, as already shown in this chapter, like to quote passages from the Bible that promote a more open and tolerant Christian faith or provide poetic support for truths or my philosophical beliefs that I believe are supported by or at least consistent with science.

So the intended meaning of Nietzsche's "God is dead" assertion that "When one gives up the Christian faith, one pulls the right to Christian morality out from under one's feet" (Hendricks 2016, para. 2) doesn't apply to me. And it needn't apply to those wishing to adopt or return to a "Christian faith" minus faith in Biblical inerrancy as well as the nuanced, paradoxical descriptions of the God and Christ found in the creeds. After all, as I learned, the Nicene and Apostle's creeds were controversially "inspired" by early fourth to seventh century men based on culture, politics, compromise, and conflicting biblical texts and passages. For those whose inspiration slightly differed? They were then heretics and often subjected to damnation (e.g., Ehrman 2014, 323–71).

My belief in God is not based on observation, logical proof, or scientific theory, which is why I must be agnostic. I feel all theists should be agnostic unless they have seen God, as should all atheists, for they should realize that their disbelief in a God is also not supported by observation, logical proof, or scientific theory. Below I give seven reasons why I can believe in a God.

A NATURAL AFTERLIFE DISCOVERED

My Rationale for a God. First, given our marvelous world, the laws that govern it, and the wonders that I am grateful to be part of and experience, I find it hard to believe in the alternative. Which is? It all just randomly materialized and evolved with no purpose, perhaps as just one of an infinite number of possible universes.

I'm well aware that any argument for a God as creator begs the question of how and why God came to exist. However, assuming no God, the mere existence of our universe or an infinite number of generated or successive universes begs the question of how and why our universe or the generation or succession process came to exist.

To me, more spectacular than the Genesis creation is how an external reality—consisting only of electromagnetic waves and particles or quantum fields (see Chapter 5), devoid of any color or life (not even a shred of genetic material)—created, by itself,

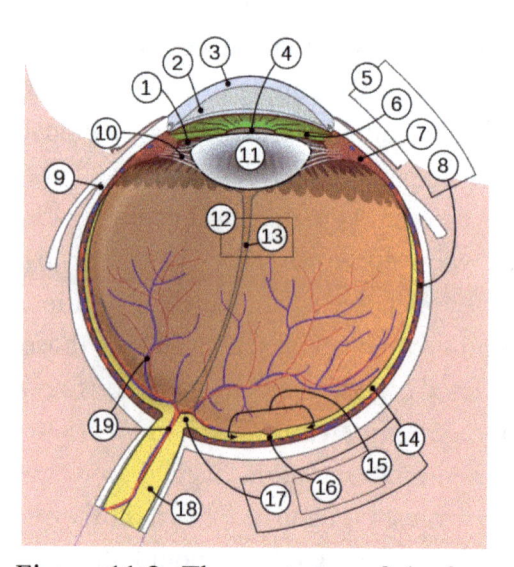

1. Posterior chamber
2. Anterior chamber
3. Cornea
4. Pupil
5. Uvea
6. Iris
7. Ciliary body
8. Choroid
9. Sclera
10. Suspensory ligament
11. Lens
12. Vitreous humour
13. Hyaloid canal
14. Retina
15. Macula
16. Fovea
17. Optic disc
18. Optic nerve

Figure 11.2. The anatomy of the human eye. Combined with our brain, it creates a spatial color pattern that is part of our sensory reality. Source: Wikimedia Commons

human sight. It somehow evolved two very complex human eyes (see Figure 11.2) and a brain to convert just the correct 0.0035 percent part of its electromagnetic wave spectrum into a spatial pattern of colors. Plus, in synch with the needed anatomy (an "input device" and "processor unit"), this inert reality also evolved the necessary conversion process (a "program") and the body (an intelligent device) that would contain it and remarkably replicate itself.[14] All of this was done to create the visual part of the sensory reality produced by our consciousness. Cosmology, chemistry, biology, and "computer science" somehow amazingly aligned!

But *why*? And how did the focus on this particular 0.0035 percent come about? Was it all achieved by this inert reality itself with no purpose "in mind" and only by many near-replications via natural selection and random DNA mutations (replication errors and environmental impacts like radiation) and genetic drift (chance mating and survival)? This may be so, but to me, more believable is that *there was some intelligence with some purpose that played some role in it*. Perhaps if only a few slight nudges along the way?

I ask you to conduct another thought experiment. Think of the probability that humankind's closest equivalent creation—the camera, microprocessor, and needed computer programs in the body of a smart device—could have been created like our visual reality from only fundamental elements and compounds. It evolved "only by many near-replications via ... random (i.e., without purpose)" changes in element and compound configuration and program code, trial and error, and selection based on being better suitable for whatever. Note that this evolutionary process would require some replication, competition, and disposal processes. Also, note that other devices might evolve along the way—e.g., an axe, an abacus, or a digital clock.

---

[14] As can be seen, much more is required than just the rod and cone cells of the retina, which are not shown in Figure 11.2 and whose evolution is speculated in (EMBL, 2004).

Knowing the complexities and permutations at play, I and I think any computer scientist would assign a near-zero probability.

The second reason I can believe in a God is that my God is mysterious—i.e., beyond complete human understanding and of an unknown nature. I don't think one needs to completely accept the God whose nature is pigeonholed by ancient legend and less knowledgeable people living in the Biblical era and early centuries C.E.

Third, given our limited consciousness, I believe it is naïve and arrogant to think that humans are the ultimate creature in body and mind as ants might also think of themselves—or, more likely, unthinkingly "assume"—given their limited consciousness. Humans are aware of only five percent of the universe. The other ninety-five percent we just label as dark energy and mass.

Fourth, my God cannot defy logic, is not necessarily all-powerful, has free will, and perhaps even makes mistakes. Indeed the Bible presents a God who makes mistakes. Apparently, God created humans thinking they would not do evil (Gen. 3) and made covenants thinking they could be kept (e.g., Gen 12:1–3, Deut. 28). Jesus (God incarnate based on the Creeds), when speaking of his second coming and its preceding tribulations, stated "Truly, I say to you, this generation will not pass away before all these things take place" (RSV, Mark 13:26–30). Well, that didn't happen.

Fifth, I believe that glimpses of God can be seen in humans. The Bible states that God created (which I interpret as evolved) them "in the image of God" (RSV, Gen. 1:27). For me, this divine image personifies the highest of evolutionary qualities—i.e., those of justice, forgiveness, grace, unselfishness, and love. Some humans exemplify such qualities much more than others. A few are driven to dedicate and even sacrifice their lives to exhibit and preach them. Religions have formed around a very select few of these individuals. Believing in a God that epitomizes such qualities gives me something to aspire to, worship, and pray to, if only in my thoughts.

Sixth, my God does not do or wish evil. I believe evil results from human intelligence, free will, and the laws of nature operating within a material world. Just like free will is logically incompatible with a utopian afterlife, it is also so with a utopian real life. Moreover, the more intelligent and thus more capable a creature, the more evil can come from their decisions. Think nuclear bombs. Low-level creatures in the evolutionary tree of life and human babies cannot do evil or even know evil. They simply know survival. And unfortunately, falling rocks can, by the laws of nature—involving mass, energy, and forces like gravity—cause bodily injury and death.

Moreover, I believe since human evolution reached the point of having eaten "of the tree of the knowledge of good and evil" (RSV, Gen. 2:17), humanity is in a race to survive. Continuing evolution in intelligence increases our "knowledge of good and evil," which then advances our technology for doing greater good or evil. Which will prevail? Will we become more evil before we become God-like and, as a result, eventually become extinct as a species? Is God only a spectator in this race, rooting for good to prevail but not interfering? Or, does God do more than root—i.e., provide some support for the good without obvious intrusion? Or, does God, in the end, decide the outcome? I would say "no" to the latter.

Regarding God as a sentencing judge, a hellish NDE need not be seen as *imposed* with a vengeance but perhaps somehow caused by oneself based on a lifetime of decisions made, memories formed, and the resulting mindset. Besides, we don't know whether any reported hellish NDE would have become a hellish natural afterlife had the person died. Sometimes, a hellish NDE has served as a "wake-up call" in this life for the NDEr. So in death, perhaps it may be just a "purgatory" for repentance before subsequent final merciful moments.

Seventh, though science progressively turns the supernatural into natural, great opportunities have existed and still do, likely forever, within the laws of nature where a God *could* be stealthily operative (i.e., as a paranormal agent). And noteworthy is that these opportunities need not interfere with free will.

Indeed, God could be operative in nature (i.e., the universe) as:

- the creator who prescribed the laws of nature with constant values finely tuned to permit the existence of life, set the evolution of the cosmos in motion, and ignited the "spark" of life that would begin its evolution;
- the infinite consciousness that existed before life existed—for without consciousness, the concept of something (e.g., a universe) is nonsensical (Ehlmann 2014);
- the decider regarding the state of a particle created by the collapse of a quantum wave function (Muller 2016; Quantum 2019);
- the mastermind behind seemingly random mutations and genetic drift that can affect life and its evolution; and
- the producer of visions, dreams, and NDEs.

Purposely left off this list is the controller of everything, which would be contrary to humans' free will.

My list assumes that God is operative *in* nature, but could God be nature *itself* if humans completely understood it? If you believe that God and nature are the same or God is partially manifested in nature, neither of which I would argue against, you are a pantheist. In his book, *The Theory of God* (which I highly recommend), astrophysicist Bernard Haisch (2009) posits a pantheism view that he argues is compatible with modern science. He states:

> It is not matter that creates an illusion of consciousness, but consciousness that creates an illusion of matter. The physi-

cal universe and the beings that inhabit it are the conscious creation of a God whose purpose is to experience his own magnificence in the living consciousness of his creation. God actualizes his infinite potential through our experience; God lives in the physical universe through us. Our experience is his experience because ultimately we are him, that is, immortal spiritual beings, offspring of God, temporarily living in the realm of matter. (137)

This view that the consciousness of God is manifested in nature was succinctly expressed long ago by a simple question:

Why do you insist the universe is not a conscious intelligence, when it gives birth to conscious intelligences? (Cicero, ca. 44 B.C.E.)

My Beliefs About an Afterlife. Given my belief in a God, what do I believe about an afterlife? For many years I've thought that one should live their life assuming no afterlife yet striving to do as God would do because it's simply the right thing to do. A heaven should not be the incentive for doing good. After all, God has no such incentive. Also, I'm grateful to God for my life and believe it extremely ungrateful to expect another—even more so, a perfect, activity-filled one. Based on the teachings of Christ, I certainly don't deserve one. Given the NEC theory, these beliefs have not changed.

Besides, I've been given the opportunity in my earthly life to feel the gratification that comes with overcoming challenges, helping others, and contributing to the world's betterment. So, what do I hope to accomplish in some eternal, already *perfect* world or make up for what I failed to do in my earthly one?

Before this theory, I believed that *if* Heaven existed, I would only get there by God's grace, and *if* Hell existed, trusting in God's grace and mercy, I need not worry. If neither Heaven nor Hell existed, I was satisfied with a before-life kind of nothingness.

Given the NEC theory, I now believe that a heaven exists and I will experience it only by God's grace and that a hell exists but trusting in God's grace and mercy, I need not worry. I no longer believe in the possibility of a before-life kind of nothingness after death. Moreover, I will be more than satisfied with an NEC that includes self and feelings over which I may have some control: peace, contentment, and gratitude. Note that the NEC theory now gives more meaning to being able to pass away on one's deathbed with these sentiments. But if I lack control of my thoughts in my last wakeful moments, or even if I don't, it will still be "into thy [God's] hands I commit my spirit" (RSV, Luke 23:46).

General Options: A Matter of Faith

Below is an exchange I had with someone who questioned how anyone could deal with the NEC theory, to put it mildly. I had answered a posted question, "Can your imagination become your afterlife?" (Quora 2018), with an affirmative answer that referenced a preprint of Ehlmann (2020). This now anonymous person replied to my answer with the comment below and then deleted it soon after I had replied, likely because his comment violated Quora etiquette guidelines. I have left out the insults and corrected some grammatical errors.

> Thanks for putting that terrifying thought in our minds, you … . Just knowing the impact it will have on those who read this, why would anyone choose to believe this? It is possible that you actually believe you can be trapped consciously in one moment for eternity. How do you think that makes those of us feel who have lost people to suicide or tragedy? So you would have us believe they are reliving moments in that frame of mind for eternity? … I'm choos-

ing to erase this from my memory and throw it in the gibberish pile.

This comment makes it clear that dealing with the NEC theory can be an obstacle to accepting it. After posting my reply, this person apologized for their rudeness, thanked me for my comments, and then deleted our exchange. My reply was:

> First, "O ye of little faith"—i.e., little trust in nature or a benevolent God. Is it nature and/or a God that often so graciously induces amnesia to erase the final terrifying moments of a tragic accident or encounter, perhaps backtracking one to a prior present moment? Moreover, do you not believe in dreams or near-death experiences (NDEs)? Both can easily override any last terrifying awake moment. Search the internet or read some of the books ... that document the many reports of people having extremely pleasurable NDEs after suffering some trauma that has put them near death. Also, don't assume everyone who commits suicide ends their life with terrifying or even unpleasant thoughts. And no matter such thoughts, dreams and NDEs can still override them.
>
> Second, believe or not in the NEC and the natural afterlife as you would believe or not in evolution by natural selection or in global warming caused by humans. These are or are not real, despite what you or I might believe. So, please don't blame me or anyone else for identifying and pointing out the empirical evidence and logic that supports them. Instead, deal with the NEC just like we all need to deal with evolution and global warming rather than sticking our heads in the sand and choosing to ignore them. Confronting new phenomena is when beliefs, perhaps based on faith, may need to be adjusted. And yes, the NEC theory may require some major adjustment in beliefs for those whose

philosophy includes a strong faith that death brings a guarantee of nothingness. Sorry, but given the NEC, our precise fate at death remains a mystery.

In the next chapter, I further discuss the NEC's impact on suicide.

Once the NEC is accepted, dealing with it requires one to answer the question, "What or who determines the content of one's last conscious moment? As this is unknown, what to believe is a matter of faith and boils down to the following three options.

1. Random chance.
2. Nature. One's nature determines it—i.e., their character, mindset, and stored memories resulting from their experiences and decisions in life.
3. God (or some other paranormal agency). A God (or something mysterious) determines it presumingly based on one's beliefs, how they've lived their life, or some combination.

If one believes in option 1, hopefully, they're an optimist. Perhaps they can find some comfort in that: science provides evidence of the brain's propensity to create NDEs (Choi 2011; Hill 2012; Lecher 2012; Stenger 2012), studies of NDEs have found that pleasant NDEs are more likely than dNDEs (Bush 2009), and some studies have shown no link between NDErs and religious affiliations (Holden, Long, & MacLurg 2009, 118–19).

However, to lessen any feeling of being hostage to random chance, it seems prudent to believe in options 2 or 3, strive to live a moral life and be kind to others, and be at peace and content with oneself at death. The latter is especially important because, with the NEC, one must live with oneself forever. For religious naturalists, who hitherto have staunchly rejected a God and an afterlife (Crosby 2008, 5), option 2 would be the natural option. However, it does not, as does option 3, permit one to trust in a benevolent agent that could offer forgiveness and grace if such would be needed (which will likely be the case for me and many others).

Alternatively, one can deal with the NEC theory by continuing to believe in the afterlife in which they have always believed. Though it may be supernatural, illogical, or both, this afterlife would override the NEC immediately at death or sometime after that. If the latter, one would wake up from the NEC (whatever its content) to Heaven, Hell, Judgment Day, reincarnation, or whatever, just as one would wake up from a dream. Thus, as stated before, the NEC theory does not conflict with traditional religious teachings about the afterlife because true believers may view it as irrelevant or some kind of afterlife way station.

Compatibility With Religious Afterlife Teachings

On the other hand, the NEC theory can be construed as supporting some of these religious afterlife teachings. Farnaz Masumian (2009) closely examines the teachings of seven world religions and concludes that they "are significantly accommodating to the NDEs described by individuals across the world" (182). She considers both the content and aftereffects of NDEs.

Below I examine the afterlife teachings of six major religions, first Christianity and then others for which I have less expertise. I venture my thoughts about how an adherent of the religion might deal with the NEC theory. Mostly I pose questions and state my presumptions instead of making assertions. Unlike Masumian, I assume that the NDE ends with death and may be the basis of an etna. Thus an etna may include some of the activities discussed by Masumian—e.g., meeting others, a lifetime review, or an out-of-body experience (OBE). An etna based on an ELDV can also include activities and meeting others.

Christianity. The New Testament provides varying and sometimes inconsistent statements about the afterlife (Ehrman 2020, xviii).

Jesus says to the criminal hanging on the cross beside him: "Truly, I say to you, today you will be with me in Paradise" (RSV, Luke 23:43). This verse is consistent with what is often proclaimed or implied at Christian funerals—i.e., that the deceased is now with God in Heaven. Such is indeed possible with the etna. However, this verse seems to conflict with other verses in the Bible that indicate believers will not go to Heaven or Hell until after Christ's second coming and the final judgment.

If Heaven and Hell are delayed until a second coming, what happens to a dead person in the meantime? Could the NEC or etna fill the gap? Perhaps as a near-nothingness and thus a kind of limbo? Or perhaps simply as the soul's spiritual ascension into Heaven (or Hell) before being joined with "the resurrection of the body," as the Apostle's Creed states. Or, perhaps as a purgatory—i.e., an atonement for life's sins via suffering and final purification before entering Heaven (Catechism 1994, 268–69)? In studying dNDEs, Bush (2009, 77) notes that dNDErs most commonly saw their dNDE as a warning, identified past problematic behaviors, and found ways "to modify their lives in satisfying ways." Of course, these dNDErs were survivors.

Perhaps there will be no second coming and accompanying bodily resurrection because God's plans have changed. My God is allowed free will and, thus, a change of mind. How can one deny God this privilege and power? Examples can be found in the Old Testament—e.g., "And the Lord changed his mind about the disaster that he planned to bring on his people" (New Revised Standard, Exodus 32:14). Moreover, the second coming did not happen when Jesus claimed it would (again, see Mark 13:26-30). Also, Jesus states, "It is the spirit that gives life, the flesh is of no avail" (RSV, John 6:63). And the Apostle Paul says that the *bodily* resurrection will instead be spiritual:

> [42] So is it with the resurrection of the dead. What is sown is perishable, what is raised is imperishable. ... [44] It is sown a

physical body, it is raised a spiritual body. ... [50] I tell you this, brethren: flesh and blood cannot inherit the kingdom of God, ... (RSV, 1 Cor. 15:42–50)

Moreover, Jesus himself contradicts what he said in Mark 13:26-30 about the second coming:

[20] Being asked by the Pharisees when the kingdom of God was coming, he answered them, "The kingdom of God is not coming with signs to be observed; [21] nor will they say, 'Lo, here it is!' or 'There!' For the kingdom of God is in the midst of you [or *within you*]. (RSV, Luke 17: 20,21)

Could this passage mean that the kingdom of God is "within you" spiritually, both in your lifetime and in death as your NEC, possibly etna? That is if you allow it.

Judaism. Views on the afterlife from Biblical times to the present have varied widely. Some entail a future resurrection of the body, and some the immortality of the soul. This should not be surprising since parts of the Hebrew Bible reflect different views on the afterlife (Shermer 2018; Spitz n.d.). Ecclesiastes (9:5) reflects the idea of no afterlife: "For the living know that they shall die; but the dead know not anything, neither have they any more a reward; for the memory of them is forgotten." The view of a resurrection of the body is reflected by God proclaiming in Ezekiel (37:13), "And ye shall know that I am the Lord, when I have opened your grave, O my people, and brought you up out of your graves." The later Jewish view that the soul alone survives death was influenced by the dualism of Descartes (1596–1650) and later philosophers. It is reflected by the phrase, "he died, his soul was gathered to his kin, and he was buried." Variations of it often appear in the Torah, where "kin" is interpreted by some to mean "the collective of the righteous dead," according to Rabbi Elie K. Spitz (n.d.). Spitz states in his article that "many Jews ... hold to the belief that some form of consciousness survives after our last breath, even though fully understanding how that's possible eludes us."

To conclude, unlike Christianity, the afterlife teachings of Judaism have not been reconciled or prescribed in creeds. Instead, Judaism puts more emphasis on one's life in this world and on using one's free will to mend it rather than on an afterlife (Schulweis n.d.). Given this, I presume most Jews, whether they might see the NEC or etna as the immortality of the soul or as filling the gap before a bodily resurrection, would not worry much about the NEC theory. Instead, they would simply put their trust in God. A view that I would second.

Islam. Views on the afterlife are quite the opposite of those of Judaism. Islam emphasizes the afterlife—a bodily resurrection, a day of judgment, a heavenly paradise, and a hell. Qur'an 29:64 states, "The life of this world is merely an amusement and a diversion; the true life is in the Hereafter." According to Islam, whether this "true life" will be paradise or hell is decided for each person by a just and merciful God. It will be based on their beliefs in the teachings of the Qur'an and the balance of good versus bad they have done during their lifetime. A belief in life after death is deemed central because "Belief in the next world instills in one the desire to do well and avoid the wrong, however costly it may be in terms of worldly sacrifices" (whyislam 2017).

Islamic teachings describe the hereafter and the events to occur in much detail (Shermer 2018, 59–61). Muslims believe that the soul separates from the body at death and enters a state called *Barzakh,* wherein one may experience a life review. A Muslim could view this state as compatible with the etna; however, I presume many Muslims will believe that any etna or just plain NEC will be immediately overridden at death.

Mormonism. Teachings on the afterlife are like that of traditional Christianity in that they include the second coming of Christ, a bodily resurrection, and a judgment day. However, unlike Christianity, yet like Islam, paradise is described in much detail and is believed to include social relationships (e.g., marriage) and other activities (BMC Team 2017) involving physical bodies. Thus, the Mormon paradise, where body and soul are reunited, would not be compatible with the heavenly etna. However, the *Book of Mormon* states, "There is a space between death and the resurrection of the body, and a state of the soul in happiness or in misery" (Alma 40:21). Could perhaps this "space" be seen as the NEC, later to be overridden?

Buddhism and Hinduism. Teachings in these religions on the afterlife (BBC Bitsize n.d.[a]; BBC Bitsize n.d.[b]; Buddhism Zone n.d.; Johnson 2020) are similar regarding their possible compatibility with the NEC theory. Most Buddhists and Hindus believe that until they attain nirvana or moksha, respectively, one's soul or consciousness will, at death, be continuously reborn (i.e., reincarnated) into another being. When one attains nirvana or moksha, there will be total contentment and no longer any suffering.

Whether rebirth is to a better or worse realm of life depends on the law of karma, which holds that one's good or bad moral actions have consequences (if not in this life, then the next). Nirvana and moksha are the god and supreme spirit realm, respectively, the highest of several realms into which one can be reborn. There are human and animal realms. In Buddhism, the lowest realm is hell; in Hinduism, it is a kind of purgatory that involves long-term suffering where a rebirth remains possible.

In both Buddhism and Hinduism, the reborn process has a mysterious transitional stage in which the consciousness of the being leaves the body before taking up a new one. Could a Buddhist or Hinduist view the NEC or etna as this transition stage? If not, they will likely view the NEC theory as irrelevant. However, studies of NDErs have shown that their NDEs, some that include a life review, often have lasting positive impacts on their lives. (IANDS 2017). One study found NDErs to have "heightened spirituality, greater care and compassion for others, diminished value of material processions, and enhanced appreciation of life" (Noyes, Fenwick, & Holden 2009). So, could the etna be seen as providing a spiritual realm or Hindu purgatory in the cycle of rebirth?

An email I received from a reader of one of my articles sheds some light on how one raised a Hindu might view the NEC. I believe it can be of interest even to the non-Hinduist.

> I came across your essay through the academia.edu site. I wanted to tell you that the essay was a new viewpoint to me, and it touched a chord.
>
> I am a medical doctor from India, and I am a Hindu by birth, although I would like to describe myself as a pagan.
>
> There is a concept in Hinduism that "one must die in Kashi" (a place called Varanasi) and one should keep chanting (or rather seeing) one's deity in all activities of wakeful life (within limits of reasonability). The idea here is that, since death can come suddenly, one should always be in a spiritual frame of mind, quite literally "God on your lips."
>
> Even today, many Hindus take up residence in Varanasi in their twilight years to await their death. This is in a positive frame of mind and probably represents a cultural thought that fits in coincidentally with your hypothesis.
>
> I found $\Delta t=0$ very intuitive, and it probably flows from "cogito ergo sum" [translation: I think, therefore I am]. (S. Govindarajan, email, June 8, 2021)

Chapter 12

Appreciating the Theory
Benefits for the Individual and Society

Clearly, the NEC theory is more likely to be appreciated if one can understand, accept, and deal with it. But is it worthy of appreciation? That is, is the reality of the NEC and the etna beneficial for an individual as well as society?

Benefits for the Individual

For the individual, the natural afterlife can be the optimal heaven. I have already made the case that it can provide the utmost eternal happiness. Events (i.e., endless change) are not necessary or even desirable. In the article "The Meanings of Life," psychology professor Roy F. Baumeister (2013) discusses the results of a study on the differences between and importance of happiness and meaningfulness in one's life. In the excerpt below, he contrasts happiness, which is present-focused and fleeting because of constant change, with meaningfulness, which is more lasting, linking past, present, and future and providing stability.

> [A sense of] Meaning is a powerful tool in human life. To understand what that tool is used for, it helps to appreciate something else about life as a process of ongoing change. A living thing might always be in flux, but life cannot be at peace with endless change. Living things yearn for stability, seeking to establish harmonious relationships with their environment. They want to know how to get food, water, shelter and the like. They find or create places where they can rest and be safe. ... Life, in other words, is change accompanied by a constant striving to slow or stop the process of change, which leads ultimately to death. If only change could stop, especially at some perfect point: that was the theme of the profound story of Faust's bet with the devil. Faust lost his soul because he could not resist the wish that a wonderful moment would last forever. Such dreams are futile. Life cannot stop changing until it ends. But living things work hard to establish some degree of stability, reducing the chaos of constant change to a somewhat stable status quo. By contrast, meaning is largely fixed. ... Meaning therefore presents itself as an important tool by which the human animal might impose stability on its world.

The natural afterlife can translate one's sense of meaning into eternal contentment at death and provide peace and eternal happiness by allowing "endless change" to finally "stop ... at some perfect point." It grants Faust's "wish that a wonderful moment would last forever." Thus, with the NEC, it can no longer be said that "Such dreams are futile." (The reader may wish to contrast the view expressed above with that expressed by the Quora responder in the previous chapter.)

Also, no longer must one place their belief and hope in a supernatural and illogical heaven. Unlike any other afterlife described in the previous section, the etna is logical and supported by human experience and cognitive science. Moreover, it requires no belief in a god or gods. For peace of mind, however, one does need to put their trust in something, option 2 or 3 in the "General Options" section of the previous chapter, to deliver in the end, if not an optimal heaven, at least a satisfying forever moment.

The NEC provides another benefit when one believes that the content of their NEC may indeed depend on the morality of their deeds and their treatment of others during their life—i.e., one's karma. It then "instills in one the desire to do well and avoid the wrong, however costly ... in ... worldly sacrifices" (whyislam.org 2017). In Christianity terms, it prods one into wanting to ensure God will judge them a sheep (the "blessed" and "righteous") rather than a goat (the "cursed") on judgment day (RSV, Matt. 25:31–46), whenever that may be. A sheep would be "you" when Jesus states, "For I was hungry and you gave me food, I was thirsty and you gave me drink, I was a stranger and you welcomed me, I was naked and you clothed me, I was sick and you visited me, I was in prison and you came to me." He goes on to state "as you did it to one of the least of my brethren, you did it to me." A goat would be you if you did not do these things.

The importance of karma, not dogmatic beliefs, is clearly conveyed by Jesus elsewhere in the New Testament. One prime example is the Parable of the Good Samaritan, where, in no uncertain terms, he answers a lawyer's question, "Teacher, what shall I do to inherit eternal life?" (RSV, Luke 10:25–37). The answer given: "You shall love the Lord your God with all your heart, and with all your soul, and with all your strength, and with all your mind; and your neighbor as yourself." The parable then makes clear that "your neighbor," here the Samaritan caregiver, is even someone you—here the Jewish victim, the lawyer, and the audience—were taught to hate.

The NEC and karma can provide a powerful "prodding iron," which religion has hitherto provided. But I believe this iron is losing its power as the world becomes more secular. I also think that doing good—i.e., living a moral life and showing love to others—leads to a better, more happy life, clearly a benefit for the individual. Moreover, making justice, in the end, more of a possibility provides not only an incentive to do good but hope for the oppressed and victimized.

Benefits for Society

The NEC is beneficial not only to the individual but also to society. I believe it's good for society when one's final fate at death—now, by default, the content of one's NEC—remains a mystery. It may stop some from committing crimes and acts of violence. Hopefully, it may cause individuals planning to shoot up a classroom or other venue to pause and ponder what final conscious moment and karmic NEC could result from such action. One can no longer take comfort in believing that "well, whatever I do in life doesn't matter in the end because when I die, I'll just cease to exist." I believe that today too many have come to such belief by the misguided notion that it is scientifically supported when it is not. On a grander scale, fear of one's NEC fate may keep an authoritarian ruler from invading another country, wreaking havoc and untold human misery. Wouldn't that be a big plus?

The article "Moralistic Gods, Supernatural Punishment and Expansion of Human Sociality" (Purzycki et al. 2016) reports on an extensive study that supports the hypothesis that "beliefs in moralistic, punitive and knowing gods" (2016, Abstract) foster cooperation and contribute to behaviors that are intended to benefit others or society as a whole. Substitute "nature"—as described in option 2 in the Section "General Options" in the previous chapter—for "gods," and I believe this hypothesis would still be true to some extent, though "moralistic" and "knowing" will need to be speculatively interpreted as "causal." Also, I think the benefits of such belief in gods, God, or nature can be partially achieved by mere belief in their possibility.

To close this last chapter, I mention another significant individual and societal benefit of the NEC theory. The general knowledge and acceptance of the NEC, even just its possibility, can result in many fewer tragic suicides. The NEC theory gives much more meaning to Hamlet's soliloquy, which many students still study in high school. Those who contemplate suicide may, like Hamlet, now pause and think, "aye," but "in that sleep of death, what dreams "may come." (See the beginning of Chapter 1.)

Suicide can no longer be viewed as the means to escape from life into "nothingness" and rid oneself of self. When someone is in a distressed state of mind where such escape and riddance seem attractive to them, they will now realize that with suicide, they will never die from their perspective. In fact, they may be paused forever in the execution of their death or perhaps in some other experience even worse. I believe the NEC theory will likely cause many to reject suicide, thus sparing those who love them from much grief. Then, they will hopefully get the help they desperately need and go on to live a happy and meaningful life. And I hasten to add that a distraught suicide victim can still end life paused in a heavenly dream or NDE and thus a glorious natural afterlife.

Not only might the NEC theory result in fewer suicides but also fewer mass shootings. Studies have shown that mass shooters have been overwhelmingly suicidal (Dunn 2019; Koerth 2022). As previously mentioned, even if not suicidal, potential mass shooters may question what their last moment, their NEC, would be if they were killed in carrying out their plan.

Epilogue
Death's Newfound Reality

> *The human mind cannot be absolutely destroyed with the human body, but there is some part of it which remains eternal.*
> —Benedict de Spinoza, *Ethics*, Book 5, Proposition 23

What led me to write this book began with my desire to write what I thought would be one last article on the NEC theory and, hopefully, get it published. The article was titled "Death's New Reality: Challenging Orthodoxy and Dealing With Our End-of-Life Illusion of Immortality." I first mentioned it in the Etna section in Chapter 2. The title could very well have been the title of this book. Its abstract, which provided my purposes for writing it, could have served as a short prologue for this book. And with minor revisions, this abstract can also serve as a concluding summary of this book, which is why I give it below (with no changes):

> In previous articles, I have identified and discussed a new reality about death—a timeless, end-of-life illusion of immortality. I focused on this illusion itself—explaining its essence, arguing for its certainty, and generally comparing it to conventional views on the afterlife. I first called it the *natural afterlife*. Then after better grasping its psychological basis and more wide-ranging possible content, I called it

the *natural eternal consciousness* (*NEC*), which makes possible the *eventually timeless, natural afterlife* (*etna*). An etna can provide utmost eternal happiness—a real (i.e., logically consistent), optimal heaven. The previous articles are mainly impersonal, for I deemed my afterlife beliefs irrelevant. This article is more personal. I discuss how I came to discover the NEC and etna and the difficulties I have experienced in getting others to understand, accept, deal with, and appreciate these phenomena, given their elusive essence and the psychological impediments inherent in challenging orthodoxy. I also reveal my religious beliefs and offer my perspective on the philosophical and religious significance and potential impact of the NEC—the new reality that now looms for all to confront. While religiously neutral, this reality may challenge your beliefs about life after death and, thus, perhaps about life.

I submitted the "Death's New Reality" article to a few journals, mostly philosophy of religion journals, but received some of the same reasons for rejections I had grown accustomed to (as given in Tables 10.1 and 10.2). But again, were these the real reasons? Here is a montage of the kind of responses I received:

Your article is clearly of interest and is accessible and readable, but it is not within the scope of this journal. We suggest it might fit better in another journal that deals more directly with [psychology of religion, human consciousness, ...].

One big obstacle the article faced was that it was too long, over fifteen thousand words, when almost all possibly suitable journals wanted less than ten thousand. So, I decided to stop "beating my head against a wall" and instead turn the article into a book, making the applicability of its abstract no coincidence. Besides, I felt a book would allow me to bypass the scholarly "gatekeepers" and present the NEC theory to the public. Then perhaps, more scholars would finally specifically address it and deal with it. A book would also allow me to consolidate the overlapping information I had published within my articles into one comprehensive source.

So I created this book from the "Death's New Reality" article. I included material from my other articles (often with some improvement) that I had only referenced or summarized in the abandoned article. I added quite a bit of new material and reorganized it all within the structure of a book—i.e., cover, table of contents, prologue, chapters, etc.

In the remainder of this epilogue, I summarize the contributions that I feel this book makes to the vast library of books that represent human knowledge. But before I do, I again admit to something I've alluded to before.

The Biggest Writing Challenge of My Life. I've found it quite challenging to *accurately* describe and scientifically make the case for the natural afterlife, NEC, and etna. Writing articles and this book about these phenomena have been more difficult than writing technical computer science articles and a computer science book (Ehlmann 2009), which demand preciseness and logical correctness. One contribution to the difficulty is that it's rare to get helpful feedback when submitting to psychological and philosophical journals, unlike in computer science. The difficulty is especially evident when gauged by the misunderstandings reflected in the feedback I have gotten from a few reviewers but mostly the general public. Concerning these, I recognize that some misunderstandings can be attributed to my writing (though I feel my explanations have improved over time) and others to the elusive adjectives needed to specify the essence of the NEC precisely. On the other hand, misunderstandings are often baffling because I feel that if one can just have an open mind and "see the forest for the trees," the concept of the NEC is quite simple, and the underlying principles are not rocket science. Indeed, I feel astonished that I had to write a whole book about it.

Contributions. Nevertheless, I feel the major contribution of the book is that it describes the NEC, natural afterlife, and etna and shows that they are not supernatural. They are natural in that they are supported by human experience and widely accepted principles in psychology within the fields of time perception and conscious perception. The book has shown the NEC and the etna it can provide to be empirically based, deducible, testable, and possibly explanatory of a purpose for dreams and NDEs. The NEC, natural afterlife, and etna radically challenge centuries of beliefs about death. The discovery of these phenomena has been long past due.

One way to view the NEC is as a scrap of leftover consciousness that gets caught in one's self-awareness and is not biodegradable. One's last conscious moment is such because, unlike all the other gazillion moments in life, its presence in the mind—i.e., in one's self-awareness—never gets supplanted by another and remembrance can never fade because forgetting takes time. Neither timelessness nor death removes it from self-awareness because both are never perceived. Therefore human-like consciousness, once embodied within time, once born, is never obliterated but only made psychologically timeless and paused when its physical embodiment is no more.

Another contribution of this book is the revelation that there's no before-life kind of nothingness after death—psychologically, no non-existence. What emerges instead, by default, is a conscious moment of some final experience, minimally including self within some context, followed only by imperceptible timelessness. Simply put, your NEC is you believing you are experiencing all that is within this experience at a point in time and never knowing otherwise. If one still protests, "But you can't *believe* you're experiencing anything because you're dead," one must answer two questions: "When did *you* stop believing?" and "Cognitively, precisely what made *you* stop?" That is, "What made *you* aware you were wrong?" or "What made *you* aware that your last experience was over?" And please note the big emphasis on each "you."

Still another contribution is that the book explains how NDEs (and ELDVs) may result in "A Natural Afterlife." Farnaz Masumian (2013), in conclusion to her article on the compatibility of NDEs with the afterlife teachings of world religions, states that "Scientific investigation of NDEs is now beginning to offer tangible evidence for postmortem survival of some as yet unknown entity in humans" (182). Later she calls this unknown entity a "postmortem consciousness" (183).

Well, the NEC provides this "postmortem consciousness," the holy grail for many NDE researchers. These researchers, however, especially those who view the NDE as an *after*-death experience, have probably only been seeking an event-filled postmortem consciousness that would be recognized as such by everyone if only living humans could peer beyond death. They never considered that the NDE could become a timeless, never-ending experience with death and, for some, an eventually timeless, yet never perceived as timeless, afterlife that materially exists *before* death but with death is perceived by and only by the dying person as eternal and thus postmortem. Simply put, the NDE results in an NEC when an NDEr does not survive.

And so, had Dr. Eben Alexander not lived to report his NDE, it would have indeed been his afterlife, his etna. It would have included all of the pleasant activities he recounts in his book (2012a) and article (2012b) and the resulting happiness. He would have never known that his NDE had become timeless with death. Whether it had occurred before or after death and exactly how it came about would have been immaterial to him.

Thus, the NEC theory provides a middle ground in the big debate regarding NDEs, discussed in Chapter 2. The staunch materialistic-minded, however, may not be pleased.

Those claiming that NDEs provide evidence of an afterlife can now point to the scientifically supported etna. Given that they will likely never be scientifically able to claim an NDE-related eternal, event-filled afterlife, the NEC and etna can be considered a significant victory.

Those claiming that NDEs are merely the brain's natural physiological response to the brain shutting down and that they provide no proof of the *commonly* envisioned afterlife (e.g., a Heaven) can continue to do so. Thus no defeat, no "egg on one's face." While they can attempt to falsify the NEC theory, as discussed in Chapter 9, until they do, they cannot scientifically deny a timeless NDE-based spiritual NEC as a reality. Nor can they scientifically deny that the creation and contents of an NDE and NEC are not influenced by some paranormal agency, as discussed in Chapter 5.

I hope this book has made another contribution, this one indirect. It is to instill in some readers a bit more open-mindedness. Admittedly, this was lurking in my mind as a tangential objective when including discussions in this book related to:

- both the two-sided debate about NDEs, where each side had relied on age-old assumptions about the afterlife, and the philosophical centuries-old debate on immortality among dualists and materialists, where assumptions never allowed the concepts of timeless, timelessness, and relativity to be considered;
- the psychological impediments one encounters in challenging orthodoxy;
- my difficulties in getting my "out of the mainstream" articles accepted by journals and theories accepted by individuals;
- my more liberal religious views about God, the Bible, the Christian creeds, and the afterlife;

- the possible compatibilities that one might see between the etna and the afterlife teachings of some major religions; and

- the dogmatic belief in "nothingness" following death, which permits reliance on death to escape any accountability in the end for one's actions or nonactions.

I believe that more open-mindedness facilitates more insight, progress, tolerance, and civility.

Related to the previous contribution, I hope the book's final contribution is that it begins an open-minded discussion of the significance and impact of the NEC theory on religion and philosophy. And more importantly, it also helps to start an internal open-minded reassessment within some individuals about life and death.

They may require this reassessment because the content of the NEC is seemingly beyond one's control, especially given ELDVs and NDEs. And so again, "Ay, there's the rub." Everyone must address the questions: "What do you believe will be the content of your NEC, and how will it be determined? Only by chance? Or, will your after-life, now an NEC by default, be determined by nature, by some supernatural agency (e.g., God), or perhaps by some combination? And, if not by chance, based on what? These questions are similar to those about the after-life that have been with humankind for millennia. Their answers still remain a mystery and thus a matter of faith.

So some might say that the NEC phenomenon changes little. *However*, it significantly upsets the status quo by eliminating any assumed guarantee of "nothingness" upon death and by now making "A Natural Afterlife" a real (i.e., non-supernatural) possibility.

I have offered in this book some general and religious-based views on how one might deal with the NEC and natural afterlife. I've given my personal religious beliefs and positions on the questions I raised above. These allow me to comfortably deal with the NEC theory and live my life accordingly.

Parting Words. However, regardless of my beliefs or anyone else's and given the NEC, it seems prudent to at least strive to develop a self that one is happy to live with *forever* and to lead a life that allows one to be content and peaceful in one's last wakeful moment. Anything beyond that involves faith and, with it, trust.

I believe faith in a just and, hopefully, merciful NEC-determiner, God or nature, is fostered by the NEC theory. Without such faith and unless an eternal optimist, one must live in dread that random chance or even a lack of faith will result in an unpleasant timeless, everlasting experience upon death.

However, I also believe that everyone should be open-minded, and thus agnostic as to what determines the content of one's NEC because, as of now, *we don't know*. I still often wake up after having one of my many weird dreams and wonder, "What the heck could have caused my brain to come up with that?"

References

Alltime10s. (2018, May 29). Alltime10s: 10 theories about the afterlife. *YouTube.* https://www.youtube.com/watch?v=NEo-hzO9s_A&ab_channel=Alltime10s

Alexander, E. (2012a). *Proof of heaven: A neurosurgeon's journey into the afterlife.* Simon & Schuster.

Alexander, E (2012b, October 8). Heaven is real: A doctor's experience with the afterlife. *Newsweek.* https://www.newsweek.com/proof-heaven-doctors-experience-afterlife-65327.

APA. (2020). APA dictionary of psychology: Hypothesis. *American Psychological Association.* https://dictionary.apa.org/hypothesis

BBC Bitsize. (n.d.[a]). Life after death: What does Buddhism teach about life after death? *BBC Bitsize.* https://www.bbc.co.uk/bitesize/guides/zfts4wx/revision/3#:~:text=All%20life%20is%20in%20a%20cycle%20of%20death%20and%20rebirth%20called%20samsara%20.&text=Through%20good%20actions%2C%20such%20as,a%20better%20future%20for%20themselves

BBC Bitsize. (n.d.[b]). Life after death. What does Hinduism teach about life after death? *BBC Bitsize.* https://www.bbc.co.uk/bitesize/guides/zhxpr82/revision/3#:~:text=life%20after%20death%3F-,Most%20Hindus%20believe%20that%20humans%20are%20in%20a%20cycle%20of,may%20exist%20in%20other%20realms

Barbato, M., Barclay, G., & Potter, J. (April 21, 2017). Letters: The moment of death. *Journal of Pain and Symptom Management, 53*(6), e1–e3. https://doi.org/10.1016/j.jpainsymman.2017.03.003

Barnett, L. (1964). *The universe and Dr. Einstein.* Signet.

Barrientos, A. with Petrozzo, K (2021, Fall). *Death and immortality* [Video]. Academa.edu. https://www.academia.edu/video/kOvqLl?email_video_card=title&pls=RVP

Baumeister, R. F. (2013, September 16). The meanings of life: Happiness is not the same as a sense of meaning. *Aeon.* https://aeon.co/essays/what-is-better-a-happy-life-or-a-meaningful-one

Bekoff, M. (2012, December 4). Do animals dream? Science shows of course they do, rats too. *Psychology Today.* http://www.psychologytoday.com/blog/animal-emotions/201212/do-animals-dream-science-shows-course-they-do-rats-too

Block, R. A. & Hancock, P. A. (2019, June 24). Time perception. *Oxford Bibliographies.* https://doi.org/10.1093/OBO/9780199828340-0123

BMC Team (2017, May 19). What does the Book of Mormon teach about the afterlife? *Book of Mormon Central.* https://knowhy.bookofmormoncentral.org/knowhy/what-does-the-book-of-mormon-teach-about-the-afterlife.

Borjigin, J., Lee, U., Liu, T., Pal, D., Huff, S., Klarr, D., Sloboda, J., Hernandez, J., Wang, M. M., & Mashour, G. A. (2013, August 27). Surge of neurophysiological coherence and connectivity in the dying brain. *Proceedings of the National Academy of Sciences of the United States of America. 110*(35). https://doi.org/10.1073/pnas.1308285110

Bradford A. (2017, July 28). What is a scientific theory? *LiveScience.* https://www.livescience.com/21491-what-is-a-scientific-theory-definition-of-theory.html

Brennan, M. (Ed.) (2014). *The A–Z of death and dying: Social, medical, and cultural aspects.* ABC-CLIO/Greenwood.

Brooks, R.A. (2010). *Fields of color: The theory that escaped Einstein.* Universal Printing, LLC.

Brown, J.R. & Stuart, M.T. (2018, July 24). Thought experiments. *Oxford Bibliographies.* https://www.oxfordbibliographies.com/view/document/obo-9780195396577/obo-9780195396577-0143.xml

Breus, M. J. (2015, February 13). Why do we dream: New insights into what really goes on when we drift into sleep. *Psychology Today.* https://www.psychologytoday.com/blog/sleep-newzzz/201502/why-do-we-dream

Brumfield, B. (2013, April 10). Afterlife" feels "even more real than real," researcher says. *CNN.* http://www.cnn.com/2013/04/09/health/belgium-near-death-experiences

Buddhism Zone (n.d.). Buddhist afterlife beliefs. *Buddhism Zone.* https://buddhismzone.org/buddhist-afterlife-beliefs/.

Burpo, T. with Vincent, L. (2011). *Heaven is for real: A little boy's astounding story of his trip to heaven and back.* Thomas Nelson.

Bush, N. E. (2009). Distressing western near-death experiences: Finding a way through the abyss. In J M. Holden, B. Greyson, & D. James (Eds.), *The handbook of near-death experiences: Thirty years of investigation* (pp. 63–86). Praeger.

REFERENCES

Catechism of the Catholic Church (2nd ed.). (1994). *United States Conference of Catholic Bishops.* https://www.usccb.org/sites/default/files/flipbooks/catechism/

Chawla, L., Terek, M., Junker, C., Akst, S., Yoon, B., Brasha-Mitchell, E., and Seneff, M. (2017). Characterization of end-of-life electroencephalographic surges in critically ill patients. *Death Studies, 41*(6), 385–392. https://www.researchgate.net/publication/313239220_Characterization_of_End_of_Life_Electroencephalographic_Surges_in_Critically_Ill_Patients

Choi, C. Q. (2011, September 12). Peace of mind: near-death experiences now found to have scientific explanations. *Scientific American Mind.* http://www.scientificamerican.com/article/peace-of-mind-near-death/

Clark, J. (2007, October 23). Has science explained life after death? *HowStuffWorks.* http://science.howstuffworks.com/science-vs-myth/afterlife/science-life-after-death.htm

Clark, Thomas W. (1995). Death, nothingness, and subjectivity. In Daniel Kolak & R. Martin (eds.), *The Experience of Philosophy.* Wadsworth Publishing. 15-20. https://www.naturalism.org/philosophy/death/death-nothingness-and-subjectivity

Cleveland Clinic (November 11, 2020). Dissociative amnesia. *Cleveland Clinic.* https://my.clevelandclinic.org/health/diseases/9789-dissociative-amnesia

Cink, Fred (2021, October 27). How many stars and planets can there be?: Answer. *Quora.* https://www.quora.com/Recently-scientists-have-shown-that-there-are-10-times-more-galaxies-in-the-universe-than-the-previously-thought-2-trillion-How-many-stars-and-planets-can-there-be/answer/Fred-Cink

Cline, A. (2019, May 13). The difference between atheists and agnostics. *Learn Religion.* https://www.learnreligions.com/atheist-vs-agnostic-whats-the-difference-248040

Cram101 Textbook Reviews. (2017). *Psychology: Core Conceptions by Philip G. Zimbardo. Edition 7, Study Guide.* Content Technologies, Inc.

Crosby, D. A. (2002). *A religion of nature.* SUNY Press.

Crosby, D. A. (2008). *Living with ambiguity: Religious naturalism and the menace of evil.* SUNY Press.

Dewey, R. A. (2017). Chapter 8: Animal behavior & cognition: Are animals conscious? In *Psychology: An Introduction.* Psych Web. http://www.psywww.com/intropsych/ch08-animals/are-animals-conscious.html

Dittrich, L. (2013, July 2). Prophet. *Esquire.* https://www.esquire.com/entertainment/interviews/a23248/the-prophet/

Dunn, L. (2019, August 11). How suicide prevention can help stop mass killers before they start shooting. NBC NEWS. https://www.nbcnews.com/health/health-news/how-suicide-prevention-may-help-stop-mass-killers-they-start-n1040836

Ehlmann, B. K. (2009). *Object relationship notation (ORN) for database applications: Enhancing the modeling and implementation of associations*. Springer.

Ehlmann, B. K. (2013a, May 30). Perhaps heaven is your never-ending dream and natural afterlife. *Owlcation*. https://owlcation.com/humanities/Perhaps-Heaven-Is-in-Our-Never-Ending-Dream-and-Natural-Afterlife

Ehlmann, B. K. (2013b, November 7). Your natural afterlife: The non-supernatural alternative to nothingness. *HubPages*. https://discover.hubpages.com/religion-philosophy/Your-Natural-Afterlife

Ehlmann, B. K. (2014, August 2). Why something vs. nothing and the essentialness of consciousness. *Owlcation*. https://owlcation.com/humanities/Why-Something-Vs-Nothing

Ehlmann, B. K. (2016). The theory of a natural afterlife: A newfound, real possibility for what awaits us at death. *Journal of Consciousness Exploration & Research*, *7*(11), 931–950. Postprint at https://www.researchgate.net/publication/311794133_The_Theory_of_a_Natural_Afterlife_A_Newfound_Real_Possibility_for_What_Awaits_Us_at_Death

Ehlmann, B. K. (2020). The theory of a natural eternal consciousness: The psychological basis for a natural afterlife. *Journal of Mind and Behavior*. *41*(1), 53–80. https://www.researchgate.net/publication/320552180_The_Theory_of_a_Natural_Eternal_Consciousness_The_Psychological_Basis_for_a_Natural_Afterlife

Ehlmann, B. K. (2022). The theory of a natural eternal consciousness: Addendum. *Journal of Mind and Behavior*. *43*(3), 185–204. Postprint at https://www.researchgate.net/publication/349702392_The_Theory_of_a_Natural_Eternal_Consciousness_Addendum

Ehrman, B. D. (2014). *How Jesus became God: The exaltation of a Jewish preacher from Galilee*. HarperOne.

Ehrman, B. D. (2020). *Heaven and hell: A history of the afterlife*. Simon & Schuster.

Elliott, M. A. & Giersch, A. (2016). What happens in a moment. *Frontiers in Psychology, 6*(1905). https://www.frontiersin.org/articles/10.3389/fpsyg.2015.01905/full

EMBL (European Molecular Biology Laboratory). (2004, November 1). Darwin's Greatest Challenge Tackled: The Mystery Of Eye Evolution. *ScienceDaily*. http://www.sciencedaily.com/releases/2004/10/041030215105.htm

Epstein, D. (2019). *Range: Why generalists triumph in a specialized world*. Riverhead Books.

Frethheim, T. E. & Beekmann, D. H. (1972). *Our Old Testament heritage II*. Augsburg Publishing House.

REFERENCES

Gilad, E. (2019, February 7). What is the Jewish afterlife like? *HAARETZ*. https://www.haaretz.com/jewish/.premium-what-is-the-jewish-afterlife-like-1.5362876

Green, C. (1968). *Out-of-the-body experiences*. Institute of Psychophysical Research, 92, 93.

Green, J. T. (1995). Lucid dreams as one method of replicating components of the near-death experience in a laboratory setting. *Journal-of-Near-Death-Studies, 14*(1). https://doi.org/10.17514/jnds-1995-14-1-p49-59.

Gregory, T. R. (2008). Evolution as fact, theory, and path. *Evolution: Education and Outreach. 1* 46–52. https://doi.org/10.1007%2Fs12052-007-0001-z

Greyson, B., Kelly, E. W., and Kelly E. F. (2009). Explanatory models for near-death experiences. In J. M. Holden, B. Greyson, and D. James (Eds.), *The handbook of near-death experiences: Thirty years of investigation* (pp. 213–234). Praeger.

Greyson, B. (2021). *After: A doctor explores what near-death experiences reveal about life and beyond*. St. Martin's Essentials.

Haisch, B. (2009). *The God Theory: Universes, Zero-Point Fields, and What's Behind It All*. Red Wheel/Weiser.

Hameroff, S. (2017a, December 6). Consciousness and anesthesia with Stuart Hameroff. *Huffington Post*. http://www.huffingtonpost.com/deepak-chopra/consciousness-and-anesthe_b_719715.html

Hameroff, S. (2017b, December 6). Consciousness and the nature of time with Stuart Hameroff. *Huffington Post*. http://www.huffingtonpost.com/deepak-chopra/consciousness-and-the-nat_b_711116.html

Harris, S (2012, November 11). Science on the brink of death. https://www.samharris.org/blog/science-on-the-brink-of-death

Hendricks, S. (2016). 'God is dead': What Nietzsche really meant. *BIG THINK*. https://bigthink.com/scotty-hendricks/what-nietzsche-really-meant-by-god-is-dead

Herzog, M., Kammer, T., and Scharnowski, F. (2016, June 7). Time slices: What is the duration of a percept? *PLOS BIOLOGY, 14*(6), 1–5. https://doi.org/10.1371/journal.pbio.1002433

Hill, K. (2012, December 3). The death of 'near death': Even if heaven is real, You aren't seeing it. *Scientific American*. http://blogs.scientificamerican.com/guest-blog/2012/12/03/the-death-of-near-death-even-if-heaven-is-real-you-arent-seeing-it/

Hoffman, J. (2016, February 2). A new vision for dreams and dying. *The New York Times*. https://www.nytimes.com/2016/02/02/health/dreams-dying-deathbed-interpretation-delirium.html

Holden, J. M., Greyson, B., & James, D. (Eds.) (2009a). *The handbook of near-death experiences: Thirty years of investigation*. Praeger.

Holden, J. M., Greyson, B., and James, D. (2009b). The field of near-death studies: Past, present, and future. In J. M. Holden, B. Greyson, and D. James (Eds.), *The handbook of near-death experiences: Thirty years of investigation* (pp. 1–16). Praeger.

Holden, J. M., Long, J., & MacLurg, B. J. (2009). Characteristics of western near-death experiencers. In J M. Holden, B. Greyson, & D. James (Eds.), *The handbook of near-death experiences: Thirty years of investigation* (pp. 109–133). Praeger.

Hsu, J. (2015, August 26). Estimate: Human brain 30 times faster than best supercomputers. *IEEE Spectrum.* https://spectrum.ieee.org/tech-talk/computing/networks/estimate-human-brain-30-times-faster-than-best-supercomputers

Hunt, H. T. (1995). *On the nature of consciousness: Cognitive, phenomenological, and transpersonal perspectives.* Yale University Press.

Hunt, H. T. (2012). Toward an existential and transpersonal understanding of Christianity: Commonalities between phenomenologies of consciousness, psychologies of mysticism, and early gospel accounts, and their significance for the nature of religion." *Journal of Mind and Behavior, 33* (1&2), 1–26 (125–150 in reprint). Reprint at https://www.academia.edu/40182026/Mysticism_and_Meaning_Multidisciplinary_Perspectives_edited_by_Alex_S_Kohav.

IANDS. (2017, December 14). Distressing near-death experiences. *International Association of Near-Death Studies, Inc.* https://iands.org/distressing-near-death-experiences.html

James, W. (1977). The stream of thought. In J. J. McDermott (Ed), *The writings of William James.* University of Chicago Press. (Originally published in 1890.)

Johnson, S. (2020, April 16). A guide to death and the afterlife in Hinduism. *Cake.* https://www.joincake.com/blog/hinduism-afterlife/

Kellehear, A. (2009). Census of non-western near-death experiences to 2005: Observations and critical reflections. In J. M. Holden, B. Greyson, and D. James (Eds.), *The handbook of near-death experiences: Thirty years of investigation* (pp. 135–158). Praeger.

Kerr, C, W., Donnelly J. P., Wright, S. T., Kuszczak, S. M., Banas, A., Grant, P. C., & Luczkiewicz, D. L. (2014). End-of-life dreams and visions: A longitudinal study of hospice patients' experiences." *Journal of Palliative Medicine. 17*(3), 296–303. https://doi.org/10.1089/jpm.2013.0371

King, R.A. (2021a). The Irrelevance of time in near-death experiences (NDEs). *Academia Letters,* Article 2427. https://doi.org/10.20935/AL2427

King, R. A. (2021b). *Differences and commonalities among various types of perceived OBEs.* The NDE OBE Research Project. https://doi.org/10.13140/RG.2.2.23418.82882/1

Koch, C. (2020, June 1). What near-death experiences reveal about the brain. *Scientific American.* https://www.scientificamerican.com/article/what-near-death-experiences-reveal-about-the-brain/

Koerth, M. (2022, June 6). Suicide prevention could prevent mass shootings. *FiveThirtyEight: abc NEWS.* https://fivethirtyeight.com/features/suicide-prevention-could-prevent-mass-shootings/

REFERENCES

Lanza, R. with Berman, B. (2009). *Biocentrism: How life and consciousness are the keys to understanding the true nature of the universe*. BenBella Books.

Lanza, R., Pavšič, M., with Berman, B. (2020). *The grand biocentric design: How life creates reality*. BenBella Books.

Le Neindre P., Bernard E., Boissy A., Boivin X., Calandreau L., Delon N., Deputte B., Desmoulin-Canselier S., Dunier M., Faivre N., Giurfa M., Guichet J-L., Lansade L., Larrère R., Mormède P., Prunet P., Schaal B., Servière J., Terlouw C. (2017). Animal consciousness. EFSA supporting publication 2017:EN-1196. https://efsa.onlinelibrary.wiley.com/doi/pdfdirect/10.2903/sp.efsa.2017.EN-1196

Le Poidevin, R. (2015). The experience and perception of time. *Stanford encyclopedia of philosophy*, E. N. Zalta (Ed.). https://plato.stanford.edu/entries/time-experience/

Lecher, C. (2012, October 10).FYI: What causes near-death experiences? *Popular Science*. https://www.popsci.com/science/article/2012-10/fyi-what-causes-near-death-experiences/

Levitan, L., & LaBerge, S. (1991). Other worlds: Out-of-body experiences and lucid dreams. *Nightlight* (The Lucidity Institute), *3*(2–3). http://www.lucidity.com/NL32.OBEandLD.html

Lewis, P.A. (2013). *The secret world of sleep: The surprising science of the mind at rest*. Palgrave MacMillan.

Lewis, P.A. (2014, July 18). What is dreaming and what does it tell us about memory? *Scientific American Mind*. http://www.scientificamerican.com/article/what-is-dreaming-and-what-does-it-tell-us-about-memory-excerpt/

Lexico. (2022). Clinical death. *Lexico: Oxford languages*. https://www.lexico.com/en/definition/clinical_death

Long, J. with Perry, P. (2010). *Evidence of the afterlife: The science of near-death experiences*. HarperCollins.

Long, J. A. (2003, March 27) Dreams, near-death experiences, and reality. *NDERF*. https://www.nderf.org/NDERF/Research/dreams_reality032703.htm.

Louie, K., & Wilson, M. A. (2001). Temporally structured replay of awake hippocampal ensemble activity during rapid eye movement sleep. *Neuron, 29*(1), 145–156. https://doi.org/10.1016/S0896-6273(01)00186-6

Low, P. et al. (2012, July 7). *The Cambridge declaration on consciousness*. Francis Crick Memorial Conference on Consciousness in Human and non-Human Animals, Cambridge, UK. http://fcmconference.org/img/CambridgeDeclarationOnConsciousness.pdf

Luo, L. (2018, April 12, 2018). Why is the human brain so efficient? How massive parallelism lifts the brain's performance to above that of AI. *Nautilus | Neuroscience*. https://nautil.us/why-is-the-human-brain-so-efficient-237042/#:~:text=But%20the%20brain%20also%20employs,convert%20light%20into%20electrical%20signals.

Manning, L., Cassell, D., & Cassell, J. (2017). St. Augustine's reflections on memory and time and the current concept of subjective time in mental time travel. *Behavior Sciences. 3*(2), 232-243. https://doi.org/10.3390/bs3020232

Martin, A. R. (2018, May 14). Brain death. *ENCYCLOpedia•com: CENGAGE.* https://www.encyclopedia.com/medicine/diseases-and-conditions/pathology/brain-death

Masumian, F. (2009). World religions and near-death experiences. In J M. Holden, B. Greyson, & D. James (Eds.), *The handbook of near-death experiences: Thirty years of investigation* (pp. 159–183). Praeger.

McNally, L., Ruxton, G. D., Cooper, N., & Jackson, A.L. (2013, October). Metabolic rate and body size are linked with perception of temporal information. *Animal Behavior. 86*(4). doi.org/10.1016/j.anbehav.2013.06.018

McNamara, P. (2014, October 14). Dreams more accurately track thought and emotion than waking. *Psychology Today.* https://www.psychologytoday.com/blog/dream-catcher/201410/dreams-more-accurately-track-thought-and-emotion-waking

Miller, L. (2010, March 25). Can science explain heaven. *Newsweek.* https://www.newsweek.com/can-science-explain-concept-heaven-69641

Mobbs, D., & Watt, C. (2011). There is nothing paranormal about near-death experiences: How neuroscience can explain seeing bright lights, meeting the dead, or being convinced you are one of them. *Trends in Cognitive Sciences, 15*(10), 447–449. https://doi.org/10.1016/j.tics.2011.07.010

Moody, R. A. Jr. (2001). *Life after life: The investigation of a phenomenon—Survival of bodily death.* Harper One.

Muller, R. A. (2016). *Now: The physics of time.* W. W. Norton & Co.

NAS. (1998). National Academy of Sciences of the USA. Teaching about evolution and the nature of science. *National Academies Press.*

Nelson, K. (2011). *The spiritual doorway in the brain: A neurologist's search for the God experience.* Dutton.

NASA. (2012, September 25). Hubble extreme deep field (XDF). *NASA HUBBLESITE.* https://hubblesite.org/contents/media/images/2012/37/3098-Image.html

Noh, E., Liao, K., M. V., Curran, T., and de Sa, V. R. (2018, July 10). Single-trial EEG analysis predicts memory retrieval and reveals source-dependent differences. *Frontiers in Human Neuroscience. 12*(258). https://doi.org/10.3389/fnhum.2018.00258

Noyes, R. Jr., Fenwick, P., & Holden, J. M. (2009). Aftereffects of pleasurable western adult near-death experiences. In J M. Holden, B. Greyson, & D. James (Eds.), *The handbook of near-death experiences: Thirty years of investigation* (pp. 41–62). Praeger.

Pachniewska, A. (2015, April 4). List of animals that have passed the mirror test. *Animal Cognition.* http://www.animalcognition.org/2015/04/15/list-of-animals-that-have-passed-the-mirror-test/

Purzycki, B., Apicella, C., Atkinson, Q. D., Cohen, E., McNamara, R. A., Willard, A. K., Xygalatas, D., Norenzayan, A., & Henrich, J. (2016). Mor-

REFERENCES

alistic gods, supernatural punishment and the expansion of human sociality. *Nature, 530* (February 10, 2016), 327–330. https://doi.org/10.1038/nature16980

Quantum. (2019, March 10). Collapse of the wave function. *Quantum Physics Lady: Encyclopedia of Quantum Physics and Philosophy of Science.* http://www.quantumphysicslady.org/glossary/collapse-of-the-wave-function/

Quora. (2018, December 3). Can your imagination become your afterlife? *Quora.* https://www.quora.com/Can-your-imagination-become-your-afterlife/answer/Bryon-Ehlmann

Ronkin, N. (2014). Abhidharma. *Stanford encyclopedia of philosophy.* Stanford University. https://plato.stanford.edu/entries/abhidharma/

Santangelo, V., Cavallina, C., Colucci, P., and Campolongo, C. (2018, July 9). Enhanced brain activity associated with memory access in highly superior autobiographical memory. *115*(30), 7795–7800. https://doi.org/10.1073/pnas.1802730115

Schulweis, Rabbi R. H. (n.d.). Afterlife: What happens after I die? *VALLEY BETH SALOM.* https://www.vbs.org/worship/meet-our-clergy/rabbi-harold-schulweis/sermons/afterlife-what-happens-after-i-die

Shaw, G. B. (2009). *Annajanska: The Bolshevik empress.* Project Gutenberg. https://www.gutenberg.org/files/3485/3485-h/3485-h.htm

Shermer, M. (2013, April 1). Why a near-death experience isn't proof of heaven. *Scientific American Mind.* https://www.scientificamerican.com/article/why-near-death-experience-isnt-proof-heaven/

Shermer, M. (2018). *Heavens on earth: The scientific search for the afterlife, immortality, and utopia.* Henry Holt and Company.

Shushan, G. (2022). *The next world: Extraordinary experiences of the afterlife.* White Crow Books.

Smith, M. (2013). *The present.* p. 2. https://archive.org/stream/pdfy-K_LjlK6E95z1j_uV/The%20Ultimate%20Truth%20%5BThe%20Present%5D_djvu.txt

Smolin, L. (2013). *Time reborn: From the crisis in physics to the future of the universe.* Houghton-Mifflin Harcourt.

Spitz, Rabbi E. K. (n.d.) Immortality of the soul. *my JEWISH LEARNING.* https://www.myjewishlearning.com/article/immortality-belief-in-a-bodiless-existence/

Stenger, V. (2012, December 11). Not dead experiences (NDEs). *The Huffington Post.* https://www.huffpost.com/entry/not-dead-expereirnces-nde_b_1957920?utm_hp_ref=weird-news&ir=Weird+News.

Stone, J. A. (2008). *Religious naturalism today: The rebirth of a forgotten alternative.* SUNY Press.

Stroud, J. M. (1955). The fine structure of psychological time. In H. Quastler (Ed.), *Information theory in psychology: Problems and methods*, 174–207. Free Press.

The Age of Ideas. (n.d.). The three stages of truth. *The Age of Ideas.* https://theageofideas.com/the-three-stages-of-truth/

Thonnard, M., Charland-Verville, V., Brédart, S., Dehon, H., Dedoux, D., Laureys, S., Vanhaudenhuyse, A. (2013, March 27). Characteristics of near-death experiences memories as compared to real and imagined events memories. *PLOS ONE.* 8(3), 1–5. https://doi.org/10.1371/journal.pone.0057620

van der Linden, S. (2011, July 26). The science behind dreaming. *Scientific American Mind.* http://www.scientificamerican.com/article/the-science-behind-dreaming/

van Dongen, P.A.M., and Vossen, J.M.H. (1984). Can the theory of evolution be falsified? *Acta Biotheoretica, 33,* 35–50. https://doi.org/10.1007/BF00045845

van Lommel, P. (2010). *Consciousness beyond life: The science of the near-death experience.* HarperCollins.

von Baer, K. E. (1862). *Welche Auffassung der lebenden Natur ist die richtige?: Und Wie ist diese Auffassung auf die Entomologie anzuwenden?* A Hirschwald.

Whyislam. (2017, October 9). Life after death. *whyislam.org: Facts about Islam.* https://www.whyislam.org/lifeafterdeath/

Zimbardo, P. G., Johnson, R. L., & McCann, V. (2014). *Psychology: Core concepts.* Pearson Education, Inc.

Zingrone, N. L. & Avarado, C. S. (2009). Pleasurable western adult near-death experiences. In J M. Holden, B. Greyson, & D. James (Eds.), *The handbook of near-death experiences: Thirty years of investigation* (pp. 17–40). Praeger.

Acknowledgments

I am grateful to my wife, Barbara Ehlmann, for graciously proofreading and finding my many stupid errors, a role she never signed on for when she agreed to marry me. I am also grateful to Ron Hartung, Mark Heidorn, and Peter D. Stone. Each carefully reviewed this book and provided helpful feedback that resulted in many improvements. I also must attribute to Ron the comment quoted in the Prologue's second paragraph.

I owe a debt of gratitude to Raymond C. Russ, PhD in psychology and editor of the *Journal of Mind and Behavior*, for supporting my work. He patiently and meticulously edited my submissions to the journal, made valuable suggestions, and found many errors. His efforts indirectly yet significantly benefited this book.

I am also indebted to Donald A. Crosby, PhD, Professor Emeritus of Philosophy at Colorado State University. He was willing to listen to a non-philosopher's radical idea of a natural afterlife, review my early articles, and give me his feedback. In assuring me that my idea was novel and possible, he gave me the confidence to continue to develop it. In stating his misgivings, he provoked me to think deeper to address them.

I want to thank Harry T. Hunt, Professor Emeritus in Psychology at Brock University, Ontario, Canada, for helping me better understand and describe his work and its relationship to mine. Also, given his cognitive psychology expertise, I appreciated and valued his review of my chapters on supporting cognitive science principles and the NEC theory "proof."

I must acknowledge Robert Lanza, MD, for opening my mind to a significantly different view of mind and matter. I recommend everyone become familiar with biocentrism.

In closing, I want to acknowledge three individuals who helped me better understand the true nature of the Bible and helped form my religious faith and philosophy. In the late 1970s, I attended Bible classes based on the book series *Our Old Testament Heritage I & II* and *Our New Testament Heritage I & II*, published by the Augsburg Publishing House. The classes were taught by Ronald N. Fritsch, who became a cherished friend and is now deceased. Soon after those classes, in Fall 1981, while at Chapman College (now Chapman University), I had the opportunity to sit in on a Philosophy of Religion class taught by Dr. Joseph Runzo. If I had not taken these classes, all excellently taught by these individuals, I would likely have never written this book. Finally, I would like to acknowledge Bart D. Ehrman. After I retired, I read several of his books on the New Testament and Christianity. Though I may take issue with a few of his opinions, his books are excellent, and I highly recommend them.

About the Author

Bryon Ehlmann was born and raised in St. Charles, Missouri. He attended Immanuel Lutheran School and graduated from St. Charles High School. In 1970, he earned his BS degree in Computer Science from the University of Missouri at Rolla (now Missouri University of Science and Technology), graduating first in his class. Awarded a National Science Foundation Fellowship, he earned his MS degree in Computer Science in 1971 from the same university. In 1992, he earned his PhD in Computer Science from Florida State University.

He worked for twelve years for Burroughs (now Unisys) Corporation doing research and development related to database management, query languages, report writing, and user interface software systems. In 1987 he was presented the Employee Exemplary Action Award for developing the menu-based user interface for the operation of Unisys large mainframe computers.

He worked for thirty years in academia, teaching courses and doing research in programming, database management, software engineering, user interfaces, discrete mathematics, and computer theory. He published thirty-two computer science peer-reviewed articles and a book about database development titled *Object Relationship Notation (ORN): Enhancing and Modeling the Implementation of Associations*. He was an Assistant Professor of Computer Science at Chapman College (now Chapman University) from 1980 to 1985. In 2012, he retired as a Full Professor from both Florida A&M University and Southern Illinois University Edwardsville.

In retirement, his main "hobby" has been reading and researching topics in psychology, philosophy, and religion. He is married, with two children and two step-children, and lives in Tallahassee, Florida, with his wife, Barbara Ehlmann.

Index

A

absolute truths, 127
activity, 3, 16, 32, 53, 58, 61, 95, 96, 110, 121, 126, 169, 170, 172, 187, 191, 192, 203
after-life, 45, 50, 51, 53, 63, 88, 110, 111, 113, 120, 152, 171, 199, 205
afterlife
   "nothingness", 14, 135, 144, 184, 197, 202, 205
   as related to God, 184
   my view, 183
   religious teachings, 187–92
   supernatural, 3, 14, 15, 17, 22, 23, 25, 45, 48, 51, 60, 88, 89, 102, 135, 152, 172, 182, 187, 202, 205
   timeless, 3, 15, 17
   time-perceiving, 23
agnostic, 171, 176, 177, 206
Alexander, Eben, 5, 21, 25, 203
amnesia, 51, 91, 185, 209
analogy, 39, 43, 45, 76, 77
Apostle Paul, 188

B

Barrientos, Alex, 78
Baumeister, Roy F., 193
before-life, 14, 45, 50, 53, 89, 110, 144, 163, 173, 183, 202
BF (brain functionality), 115, 143, 144, 146, 147
Bible, 177, 180, 188, 189, 204
   inerrancy, 177
   Sermon on the Mount, 177
   the sheep and the goats, 195
biocentrism, 27, 35, 72
Book of Mormon, 191, 208
brain death, 103, 135, 144
brain functionality, 15, 114, 115, 136, 140, 143, 144
Buddhism, 191
Burpo, Todd, 21

C

Christian creeds, 177, 204
Christianity, 187, 190, 191, 195
Clark, Thomas W., 88
class diagram, 123, 124
clinical death, 61, 112
cognitive science, 2, 4, 20, 30, 37, 49, 73, 160, 195
computer analogy, 76, 137
conscious moment, 4, 15, 30, 48, 54, 202
conscious moments, 54

conscious perception, 30, 47, 53, 54, 97, 128, 133, 147, 202
consciousness, 4, 15, 48, 49, 54, 202
Crosby, Donald A., 88, 186, 209, 217

D

Data Flow Diagram. *See* DFD.
Death and Immortality lecture, 78
Descartes, René, 81, 189
DFD (data flow diagram), 68, 69
dNDE (distressing NDE), 92, 162, 186, 188
Doctrine of Flux, 84
dream, 1, 5, 13, 14, 16, 20, 23, 26, 28, 29, 30, 39, 40–2, 44, 45, 48, 50, 52, 54, 61, 62, 64, 69, 70, 72, 75, 85, 86, 87, 91, 92, 98, 100, 101, 110, 112, 113, 118, 120-3, 131, 132, 134, 141, 142, 146, 160, 162-5, 171, 172, 182, 185, 187, 194, 202, 206
dying person
   definition, 15

E

Ehlmann, Barbara, 217
Ehlmann, Bryon (the author), 14, 18, 26, 29, 31–4, 42, 73, 129, 153, 154, 163, 165–7, 171, 182, 184, 201, 210, 215, 219
Ehrman, Bart D., 175, 177, 187, 210, 218
ELDV (end-of-life dream or vision), 16, 18, 29, 32, 86, 90, 91, 100, 110, 170, 172, 187, 203, 205
empirical truths, 127, 128, 133
end-of-life dream or vision. *See* ELDV.
end-of-life illusion of immortality, 15, 61, 199
Epstein, David, 8
eta (eventually timeless afterlife), 32, 60, 96, 170

eta principle for a perfect afterlife, 32
etna, 152
etna (eventually timeless, natural afterlife), 2, 3, 5, 8, 9, 16, 17, 19, 32, 58, 60, 63, 85, 86, 94–6, 99, 119, 121, 123, 125, 152, 170, 172, 187–93, 195, 200-3, 205
event, 23, 27, 32, 44, 45, 48, 49, 50
   examples, 50
   imperceptible, 52, 53, 59, 113, 118, 120
   perceived, 48, 50
eventually timeless afterlife. *See* eta.
eventually timeless, natural afterlife. *See* etna.
evil, 95, 180, 181, 209
evolution, 6, 20, 33, 64, 88, 101, 128, 140, 145, 153, 160, 178–80, 180-2, 185
   natural selection, 140, 160, 179, 185
   theory of common descent, 145
experience, 48, 58, 93, 110

F

false analogy, 77
faulty (of false) analogy, 43
free will, 94, 95, 99, 170, 180, 181, 182, 188, 190
Fritsch, Ronald N., 218

G

God, 3, 78, 92, 96, 100, 161, 170, 176, 177, 183–6, 188, 189, 190, 192, 204, 205
   a rationale for existence, 177–83
   image of, 180
Greyson, Bruce, 16, 42, 70, 71, 86, 87, 92, 97, 132, 208, 211, 212, 214, 216

INDEX

H

Haisch, Bernard, 182
hallucination, 16, 23, 29, 64, 70, 85, 86, 91, 100, 114, 121
Hameroff, Stuart, 44
Hamlet, 13, 34, 162, 170, 197
Hartung, Ron, 1, 217
heaven, 2, 3, 4, 21, 22, 24–6, 31, 34, 42, 89, 94–6, 99, 183, 184, 187, 188, 191, 193, 200
heavenly, 5, 16, 25, 42, 61, 63, 89, 91, 94–6, 190, 191
Heidorn, Mark, 217
hell, 2, 31, 34, 163, 164, 183, 184, 187, 188, 190, 191
hellish, 16, 89, 91, 92, 162, 181
Hill, Kyle, 21, 24, 102
Hinduism, 191, 192
Hubble XDF (eXtreme Deep Field), 176
human eye anatomy, 178, 179
Hume, David, 83, 84
Hunt, Harry T., 35–38, 212, 217
hypothesis. *See* scientific hypothesis

I

illusion, 3, 15, 30, 36, 37, 57, 61–3, 113, 136, 172, 199
immortality, 11, 17, 62, 78, 80–4, 93, 189, 190, 204, 207, 215
   definition, 80
   dualist view, 80–3
   holistic view, 80–2
   Homeric view, 81, 82
   materialist view, 80–3
   meaning, 79
Imperceptible Death, 134, 135
Imperceptible Loss of Time, 130–2, 135, 144
Islam, 190, 191

J

Jesus, 188
Job, 174
Judaism, 189, 190

K

karma, 191, 195
kitchen, 69
   thought experiment, 71–72
Koch, Christof, 34

L

Lanza, Robert, 27–9, 65, 72, 172, 213, 218
life review, 61, 92, 190
lifetime-in-eternity model, 21, 27, 52, 59, 109, 111, 115, 123, 146
Long, Jeffrey, 23, 165
lucid dreams, 72

M

Masumian, Farnaz, 187, 203
Miller, Lisa, 25
$minBF_{nde}$ event, 115
Moody, Raymond, 22
Mormonism, 191

N

natural afterlife
   detailed definition, 93
   general definition, 16
   in a nutshell, 18
natural eternal consciousness. *See* NEC.
NDE (near-death experience), 5, 6, 16, 18, 20–6, 29, 30, 32–7, 42, 45, 50, 58, 6–4, 69, 70, 75, 85–98, 100–4, 110, 112–5, 118, 120–3, 131, 132, 134–6, 140, 142, 143, 146, 155,

157, 158, 162, 166, 171, 172, 181,
182, 185-7, 192, 202-5
NDEr (near-death experiencer), 16, 22,
23, 61, 62, 86-9, 91, 92, 93, 97,
137, 162, 186, 192, 203
NDNIV, 84
near-death experience. *See* NDE.
near-death experiencer. *See* NDEr.
NEC (natural eternal consciousness)
    definition, 5
    elusive properties, 60
    formal definition, 119
    production speed, 61
    time distortion, 62
NEC notation, 59, 115, 117, 119, 123,
126, 137
NEC theory
    essentially stated, 14
    formal statement, 30, 133
    logically stated, 134
NEC_{FD} (NEC formal definition), 119,
120, 121, 132, 133-5
NED (never-ending dream), 26, 27, 29
NED theory, 26, 27, 29
NEE (never-ending experience), 29-31
NEE theory, 29
never-ending experience. *See* NEE.
Nietzsche, 177
Nirvana, 191
Nixon, Gregory M., 165
nonhuman animals. *See* other
    creatures.
nothingness, 50

O

OBE (out-of-body experience), 70, 86,
87, 92, 187
open-mindedness, 204-6
other creatures, 97, 99, 128
out-of-body experience. *See* OBE

P

P1 (philosopher 1), 75, 171
P2 (philosopher 2), 171
P3 (philosopher 3), 63, 171, 172
palliative care, 16, 103, 104
pantheist, 182
paranormal agency, 69-71, 91, 92,
100, 186, 204
paused consciousness in timelessness.
    See PCT.
PCT (paused consciousness in
    timelessness), 32, 33, 129, 130,
    131, 133, 134, 136, 140-2
PCT theory
    "proof", 130
    formal statement, 33, 130
    logically stated, 130
Petrozzo, Katie, 79
philosophy of mind, 79
philosophy of religion, 79
Plato, 81, 83
present moment, 15, 48, 55
psychological time, 51, 52
psychological timelessness, 51, 109
purgatory, 182, 188, 191, 192

Q

Qur'an, 190

R

railroad diagrams, 118
reality
    external, 65-7, 69, 71, 72, 86
    non-sensory, 68-71, 85, 120
    physical, 27, 28, 65, 67, 86
    sensory, 65, 66, 67, 69, 70, 71,
    110, 120
reincarnation, 191
Runzo, Joseph, 218
Russ, Raymond C., 165, 217

INDEX

S

scientific hypothesis, 128, 134, 138
scientific theory, 9, 30, 49, 99, 101, 128, 129, 138, 140, 177
self-awareness, 18, 56, 73, 77, 78, 136, 137, 141, 144, 202
sense of motion, 55
sense of self, 15, 42, 44, 50, 54, 55, 89, 100, 112, 120, 152
sense of time, 44, 50, 55, 59, 152
    flow of time, 55
    passage of time, 55
Shakespeare, William, 13, 14, 20
Shermer, Michael, 23
Shushan, Gregory, 16, 105
soul, 42, 79, 81, 82, 84, 188–91, 194, 195, 215
state diagram, 110, 111, 118
Stone, Peter, 217
stream of consciousness, 4, 91, 115, 119
suicide, 97, 184, 185, 197
survival hypothesis, 105

T

theory. *See* scientific theory.
theory of a natural afterlife, 29, 153, 154, 156, 162, 165
theory of a natural eternal consciousness. *See* NEC theory
theory of common descent analogy, 145
theory of paused consciousness in timelessness. *See* PCT theory.
thought experiment, 39, 40
time, 3, 14, 15, 27–9, 37, 41, 44, 48, 49, 51, 62
time perception, 30, 47, 50–3, 62, 202
timelessness, 50, 52, 53, 55, 58, 118, 119, 120, 122, 126, 132, 134, 136, 141–3, 202
time-perceiving consciousness, 43
Torah, 189

V

van Lommel, Pam, 23
vision, 16, 29, 85, 86, 182
vital-organ failure event, 112

CPSIA information can be obtained
at www.ICGtesting.com
Printed in the USA
LVHW050343240623
750644LV00001BA/1

9 798218 175818